The Content Strategy MasterClass

The official guide to get the most out of your content marketing investment (at WriterAccess and beyond) with the latest content strategy methodology and technology to grow your business.

Byron White
CEO and Foun~~
Chair, Conten~

~
Content Mar~
Professional Writing ~~u *Price Guide*
Top 139 Content Marketing Tools

Author
Byron White

CEO, WriterAccess
Chair, Content Marketing Conference

All inquires should be addressed to:

WriterAccess
205 Portland Street Suite 500
Boston, MA 02114

http://www.writeraccess.com

International Standard Book Number: 978-1-60275-060-9

This book is intended for use as an informational guide and entertainment purposes and should not be used as a substitute for any professional medical care or treatment, professional legal advice or professional financial guidance.

CONTENTS

Executive Summary

Let's face it. The traditional marketing and sales funnel is no longer relevant in today's marketplace. Push marketing tactics simply don't work. Cold calling is dead. Customers no longer want to be sold to in the traditional buy-sell mode.

Content marketing is what's new, and what's next. Yet the practice, methodology and technology that make up the art and science of this growing industry are all at early stages of development.

The Content Strategy Masterclass book will teach you the essentials of content content strategy that make content marketing perform. You'll learn new tactics and products to aim your content marketing in the right direction, so you can deliver on performance goals.

Here's a quick top-line view of what you'll learn:

- How to develop content strategy to achieve your goals
- The best content tactics to achieve results
- How to measure performance along the way
- How to adjust strategy based on performance
- How and why all departments need to play a role
- How to convince your boss to invest in content marketing

You'll see that the Masterclass book combined with WriterAccess tools and resources will give you the methodology and technology you need to craft content strategy to grow your business or clients business organically—the content marketing way!

Online Courseware and Certification at WriterAccess

The MasterClass book comes with comes with lots of online resources including templates, videos, podcasts and webinars that are referenced throughout the course. We've also setup an online Content Strategy MasterClass portal offering certification for completion of the program.

But to access all the resources and certification, you'll need an account to officially fortify your smartitude and advance your career.

WriterAccess My Tools. When you log on to WriterAccess, visit My Tools in the left column for access to more than a dozen tools that you'll be using with the Masterclass, referenced throughout this book called WriterAccess MY Tools.

Growth Library. You'll also find a Growth Hub and Growth Library at WriterAccess—the nerve center for lots of resources including videos, templates, proposals, content plans and more, referenced throughout this book called WriterAccess Growth Library.

Content Marketing Conference Videos. We recently launched the video recordings from our Content Marketing Conference including 11 keynotes and 35 sessions covering content marketing a to z, available to all WriterAccess customers.

About WriterAccess

Before we launched WriterAccess in 2010, we ran a full-service content marketing agency serving bigger brands like Walmart, The Company Store, SalesForce, Iron Mountain, and dozens of others. To help our agency stand out from the competition, we developed our own proprietary software called WordVision (WordVision.com) that tracks the impact of content we've created, optimized, and published for clients. WordVision was our "secret sauce" to earning the trust of clients, delivering (and tracking) the performance they demanded for their investment.

We moved away from the agency model in 2010 to focus on WriterAccess — an online marketplace connecting clients directly with professional freelance writers, editors, translators, and content strategists. Working with big budgets was exciting, but scaling was difficult and turning our backs on small businesses was not in our DNA. So we ported our 100 clients over to WriterAccess, and zoomed from 100 to 25,000 customers organically in less than 5 years, without VC funding for growth.

We've learned a lot by creating and publishing more than one million content assets to date. And we're always asking our customers and freelancers how we can make WriterAccess better. And even better than that. Here are the two pain points that have surfaced:

- Customers #1 Challenge: Access to the freelance content strategists that can quickly develop strategy and deliver pre-defined products that will deliver performance goals.

- Strategists #1 Challenge: Certification for the latest tactics, techniques, and technology, as well as strategic software to work with clients and a community forum to share ideas.

To help WriterAccess customers with these challenges, we decided to create a Growth Partner program with a mission help businesses and agencies grow their business and advance their career with training, tools and support. We launched a new My Tools section of WriterAccess featuring research tools, journey mappers, persona builders, topic research tools, content planner, StyleMetrics Matcher and more. And we created the opportunity for customers to contract and hire Content Strategists in the platform to "work together" to forge content strategy and achieve goals.

The Content Strategy Masterclass book is one of the rewards we offer WriterAccess customers, and our growth partners, along with growth consultations quarterly to review reports and ideas for betterment, both with their strategy and tactics, and new tools we dream up to make the workflow better.

Even if you're not a WriterAccess customers, this book will teach you how to master that artistic and scientific content strategy to power content planning, creation, optimization, distribution and performance goals.

Content strategists, content managers, WriterAccess customers — Everybody wins!

About the Author

Way back when the web was in diapers, I started my second company called LifeTips with a vision to make life smarter, better, faster and more fun. In five years, we managed to publish 120,000 tips, 50+ books and 300+ podcasts. All this content attracted millions of readers, listeners and fans, thanks to the many freelancers we worked with and a team of content strategists, editors and SEO specialists who helped us forge new ground with content marketing.

But it was hard to compete in the publishing world on a shoestring budget. So in 2005, we leveraged our experience and started a new company, a full-service content marketing agency that quickly grew to serve 100+ customers such as WalMart, The Company Store, SalesForce, Iron Mountain, LowerMyBills and many others. We also launched new methodology and technology that were put to the test by large-scale budgets and our clients' performance demands for content marketing.

All that was exciting, and we exceeded expectations with just about every client. But I found the agency business difficult to scale. And we did not have the bandwidth to service smaller businesses in need of quality content and solid strategy to fuel the content marketing revolution.

So in 2010, we launched a cloud-based platform called WriterAccess, capable of connecting thousands of customers directly to thousands of professional writers, editors, translators and content strategists. Our success with WriterAccess has proven to be nothing short of incredible, attracting almost 25,000 customers and 14,000 freelance writers, with nearly a million projects completed.

The company is self-funded and has grown organically without venture capital. We made the Inc. "5,000 List of Fastest Growing Companies" for the last three years in a row and continue to thrive.

Our catbird seat at WriterAccess now allows us to study what customers order, how they order it, and how writers deliver the quality they demand. We're in a great spot to help the industry establish a baseline for what to expect when you pay more for content, and what best practices to launch along the way.

To help WriterAccess customers, writers and fans stay on top of the latest methodology and technology, we launched the Content Marketing Conference in 2015. Now a leading content marketing event, CMC gathers hundreds of practitioners, industry experts, writers and thought leaders to share what's new and what's next in content marketing.

The Content Strategy Masterclass book continues the goals of CMC, helping customers and writers get on the same page with the latest content marketing methodology and technology. You'll find lots of resources from friends and thought leaders who are helping to lead the content marketing revolution in the right direction — UPWARD!

CONTENT STRATEGY OVERVIEW
and the **CUSTOMER JOURNEY**

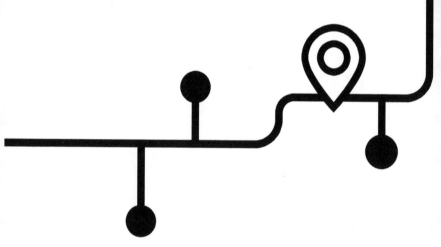

CONTENT STRATEGY OVERVIEW
and the **CUSTOMER JOURNEY**

The demand for content has never been greater. Companies in all industries have realized that compelling content is the way to connect with the readers they most want to reach. Companies, agencies and marketers of all kinds are joining the content marketing revolution in droves. But creating the right content at the right time and place is a huge challenge. The big question is: Where's all this great content — the driver for content marketing success — going to come from? How are we going to fuel the content marketing revolution?

The answer is content strategy. Content strategy is the process of planning, developing and managing content to meet strategic goals. Content strategists are the ringleaders — orchestrating all the moving parts so that they form a coherent whole. Content strategists focus on **people and process**. Understanding people — their state of mind, aspirations, inspirations and human qualities — helps us predict activity and enhance conversion and sales. Defining process — how to reach the right people at the right time, with information they want and need — allows us to achieve goals in a systematic way.

If you're a content creator or are responsible for creating content and content strategy that delivers results for a company, this workbook is for you. You'll learn not only the six steps of content marketing but also the tools and techniques to master each one. By the end, you'll have the skills to be a crackerjack content strategist for any size organization in any industry and to drive that organization's content marketing performance.

Why Content Marketing Is Essential
(It's All about the Web)

Since the launch of the first web browser in 1990, we've become more able to find the content we want — and filter out the content we don't. To connect with an audience, companies must be on the "wanted" list as sources of "must-have" information, news and entertainment. If not, they will be victims of content filtering rather than victors.

Take one look at the history of content marketing, and you'll see how quickly this new industry surged into the mainstream, led by Google and the Content Marketing Institute. Brands must now meet buyers' demands for personalized, super-useful content.

More information about the web and content marketing can be found in the WriterAccess Growth Library at the end of the workbook.

What's a Content Strategist
(and Why Do I Need One)?

Content marketing has come a long way. Content marketing is defined as the art of listening to customers' wants and needs, and the science of delivering it to them in a compelling way. We now realize that "content" must come first if the "marketing" part is to succeed. The challenge in jumping into content marketing is to get the return you demand for your investment. That's where content strategists come in.

A content strategist is the driver of a successful content marketing initiative, working diligently to aim content marketing in the right direction to achieve goals. As the popularity of content marketing rises, the need for knowledgeable content strategists is booming, as can be seen from the following figures:

• 88 percent of B2B marketers in North America use content

marketing (MarketingProfs)
- 76 percent of marketers are increasing investment in content marketing (Curata)
- 60 percent of marketers create at least one piece of content each day (eMarketer)
- Only 30 percent of marketers say their organization is effective at content marketing (CMI)

Content strategy remains relatively uncharted territory, so in a sense a content strategist is a pioneer — part of the growing content marketing revolution. The number of marketing channels is exploding. And the channels are cluttered. This course offers a road map for content strategists to win the war of words on the web.

First, we'll look at the three big challenges facing any content strategist:

- Where do you start?
- What is your goal?
- How will you get there?

Where Do You Start?

Many companies jump into content marketing by simply cranking out lots of content, hoping to engage customers and generate leads with sheer volume. This approach can best be described as "putting the cart before the horse," or, more specifically, putting content tactics before content strategy. These companies invest valuable resources into generating a large quantity of content, without first developing a strategy to identify audience needs and interests and set priorities. As a result, they contribute to content clutter and risk overwhelming consumers with too much information.

The challenge for content creators is to gain consumers' trust with a well-defined content strategy that clearly outlines objectives, terms, and roles and responsibilities without drowning them in content. The days of tricking search engines by cranking out a high volume of content are long gone. You need a map to make your way past the competition to get where you want to go.

Take a look at these stats:

- 70 percent of marketers lack a consistent or integrated content strategy. (Altimeter)
- 211 million pieces of online content are created every minute. (MarketingProfs)
- More than 2 million blog posts are published every day. (DemandMetric)
- 43 percent of consumers ignore future communications from a brand once they have received irrelevant information or products. (Gigya)
- 20 percent of consumers report they stopped buying products from a company after receiving irrelevant communications. (Gigya)

Content strategy defines the aim of content marketing and the results you should expect when you hit the target. Content strategy can be simple or complex, depending on the goals you have for content marketing. We're going to look at both ends of the strategy spectrum in this course to give you the full lay of the land, applicable to any business of any size. If you're working at a large company, you'll learn valuable insider tips. If you're a one-up agency or consultancy helping customers, you'll leave with ideas to help you scale.

What Is Your Goal?

Without lead generation, marketing fails. However, acquisition alone does not accurately measure the success of a content marketing program. Retention of customers is becoming a strategic necessity for content marketers because of the lifetime value that those customers represent. It's a lot more expensive to acquire new customers than it is to retain them, as the statistics below bear out. That realization is helping lead this new charge.

- 44 percent of companies have a greater focus on customer acquisition vs. 18 percent that focus on retention. (Invesp)
- It costs five times as much to attract a new customer than to keep an existing one. (Invesp)
- Increasing customer retention rates by 5 percent increases profits by 25 percent to 95 percent. (Invesp)

Out with the Old: The Sales Funnel

Many companies are "stuck" on sales funnel metrics designed to measure conversions and revenue. If you polled a random sample of marketing directors, you'd find many who continue to create much of their content centered on the features and benefits of their products and how "great" the company is in comparison with the competition. The sales funnel puts products and services at the heart of the conversion, which is a big mistake.

A telling example that illustrates where this problem starts is the "onboarding" of new employees to a company. Typically, step one is to educate them on products and services, to see "what we do" and "how we do it" with sales, and why customers buy from us instead of the competition. The thinking is that the faster we get up to speed on all the products and services, the sooner we can get out there and start selling or marketing them. This traditional sales funnel approach — centered on sales and marketing products or services — makes no sense, as we'll see.

In with the New: The Customer Journey

The new funnel for content marketing focuses on the customer at the center of the funnel, not on the products and services. This model relies on identifying the needs and interests of your customers and meeting them with content at those touch points.

Under this model, instead of learning about products and services, new employees learn about the core values of the company and about how the customer experience, enhanced throughout the entire customer journey, drives sales and revenue. This approach shows how informative content, presented to readers at the right place and time throughout the customer journey, moves them through the funnel. Each phase represents a point of the customer's experience with your company.

Who Owns the Customer Journey?

As one of the original content marketing revolutionaries who began writing and speaking on this topic more than a decade ago, I'm pleased to report that the revolution has been successful. But confusion still exists today as to who "owns" the customer experience throughout the journey. Is it marketing, sales, customer service or product development? Who has the experience to tap into human psychology to increase clicks, reads, social shares, purchases and referrals?

While the debate continues as to what is the best answer to these difficult questions, it seems to me that the content strategist is in the best position to answer these questions, and orchestrate the team members around a solution that centers on the Customer Journey Map. Content strategists plan and design customer experience, developing content assets that deliver on performance goals.

Starbucks, Zappos, Sephora and many other companies have a single person responsible for meeting this challenge who is known variously as the "Chief Digital Officer," "Chief Customer Officer," or "Chief Experience Officer," among the titles used. They have customer experience design skills to deliver a desired experience throughout every channel, every screen and every step of the customer journey.

Starbucks
Customer Experience Design

Take a look at the About page on the Starbucks site, mentioned in Brian Solis' fabulous book called "X: The Experience when Business Meets Design":

"It happens millions of times each week — a customer receives a drink from a Starbucks barista — but each interaction is unique. It's just a moment in time — just one hand reaching over the counter to present a cup to another outstretched hand. But it's a connection. We make sure everything we do honors that connection — from our commitment to the highest quality coffee in the world, to the way we engage with our customers and communities to do business responsibly. From our beginnings as a single store over forty years ago, in every place that we've been, and every place that we touch, we've tried to make it a little better than we found it."

As Brian notes, these carefully crafted words showcase customer experience design. Sure, Starbucks sells coffee to customers. But this language articulates the personal connection that Starbucks wants its employees to have with customers. This "experience" of connection becomes a catalyst for repeat transactions. Starbucks sales reps are viewed as "baristas" for the connection — "this cup of coffee was brewed just for you." In this simple, hand-to-hand transaction, you see sales, customer service and marketing all working together within the never-ending customer journey. Content strategists plan and design customer experience, developing content assets that deliver on performance goals.

The Customer Journey Map

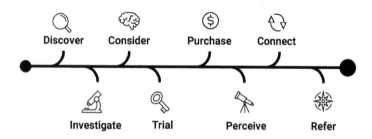

The Customer Journey Map is a document that aims to unify all team members in the marketing, sales and customer success departments to deliver a better customer experience. The content strategist is the ringleader who starts by mapping out the customer journey with various touch points that are managed by each department.

The goal is to document the valuable, personalized experiences of customers throughout their journey, and map out the content that customers can access to engage them and move them along. In this new experience-driven funnel, the customer journey never ends. There is continual and consistent tracking of results, including such goals as decreasing user acquisition cost, improving conversion rates, increasing lifetime value and many others. It's up to the content strategist to get the right information to the right people at the right time for the new customer experience funnel to be successful.

The Customer Journey Map and the Content Strategists

Rather than focusing on acquisition, lead generation or even conversion, the next-gen content strategist focuses on developing a full understanding of the customer journey gained by documenting the customer experience at various touch points along the way. Developing a Customer Journey Map becomes the first step for all content strategists, documenting how customers feel about the information they are learning, and how that information matches their needs and the company's brand, products, services and approach to marketing.

Customers need to be continually presented with content that connects and engages them for particular experiences they are feeling throughout the journey. The content strategist's role is to bring together sales, customer service and marketing to identify the path, the touch points and the content to be provided along the way.

Customer Research

The first step for a content strategist's development of a Customer Journey Map is to "get under the skin" of customers and document their pain points, wants and needs at each stage of the journey. Below are a few hacks to help remove the guesswork and find the answers. Try them all to find the nuggets of wisdom that will likely surface along the way.

- **Search Box.** Track what prospects are looking for and what they find.
- **FAQ.** Review what customers ask for and the language used.
- **Customer Service Reps.** Learn the FAQ and knowledge requests.
- **Customers.** Speak with customers and learn their wants and needs.
- **Analytics.** Discover the source of traffic and navigational pathways.
- **Surveys.** Ask for feedback on your content, navigation and methodology.
- **Help Desk Tickets.** Research the pain points that your customers experience.
- **Amazon Customer Discussions.** Research customer forums and feedback.

Conclusion: The Customer Journey Map

The Customer Journey Map documents what customers are thinking and feeling at different stages of their journey with your company, as they explore your brand, products and/or services. It also maps content topics to those needs in each stage of their journey. The map may vary from 3 to 8 stages, depending on your content strategy, journey complexity and marketing goals. Developing a Customer Journey Map helps internal team members and creative resources (freelancers) better understand how to "walk in the shoes" of customer at each stage of the customer journey, and develop better content assets that will engage them and progress them along their journey. This map is jointly created by customers and a content strategists, tasked with documenting the customer journey that services as a GPS for content marketing, featuring topics ideas for content planning that can be considered and tested for performance.

Are you ready to create a Customer Journey Map?

Discover
Marketing Assets: Webinars, Informational Guides, Podcasts, Blog
Sales WOW: Live Chat

Investigate
Marketing Assets: Explainer Videos, Competitor Comparison Chart, Webinars, Case Studies
Sales WOW: Free Platform Demos On Demand

Consider
Marketing Assets: Monthly Newsletters, Case Studies, Price Guide, Testimonials
Sales WOW: Custom Platform Features Demo

Trial
Marketing Assets: Personalized Writer Spotlights

Sales WOW: Content Analytics Setup, Book Mailed to Customers with Personal Note

Customer Service WOW: Writer Recommendations, First Order Review/Discuss

Purchase

Marketing Assets: Book 1 Mailed to Customers with Personal Note

Sales WOW: API Integration Setup

Customer Service WOW: New Talent Spotlights (Customized)

Connect

Marketing Assets: Book 2 Mailed to Customers with Personal Note

Sales WOW: Content Analytics Setup

Customer Service WOW: Writing Style Contests

Refer

Marketing Assets: Book 3 Mailed to Customers with Personal Note, Referral Program, Influencer Marketing Program

Sales WOW: Referral Green Carpet Program

Customer Service WOW: Platform Betterment Discussions/Actions, Voice of the Customer

CERTIFICATION REQUIREMENT:

In a Nutshell

Open your WriterAccess MasterClass account and download the sample customer journey map we've provided as a guide for you to follow. Then dive into the Journey Mapper at WriterAccess featured under My Tools and Planning. You're exercise is to create a customer jouney map for your business or a client's business, saving it so it's ready to use for future orders, specifying for a writer which "stage" the content will be created for to help writers understand what customers are "thinking and feeling" at that stage.

Exercise

Follow these steps to create your own Customer Journey Map that documents what customers are thinking and feeling at each touch point in their journey, ranging from awareness to consideration, to purchase to experience and referral and beyond.

1. Download Sample Customer Journey Map
2. Create Your Own Journey Map
   - Visit My Tools at WriterAccess
   - Click on Planner: Journey Mapper
   - Create Your Journey Map and Save It

Certification Test

Then take the online Customer Journey Map Test.

Helpful Tip

You'll need to tap several departments that face customers to find the answers about how customers think and feel. The sales and marketing departments will certainly have plenty of answers, particularly concerning "touch points" and "pain points" you will discover. But that's just the beginning, really. Tap customer service if you can, including Help Desk Tickets or phone support for answers to questions you've developed to harvest the right information.

Goal of the Customer Map

Your goal is to document the customer journey and experiences customers have with your brand, and then to develop topic ideas for content assets that can be put in front of the right people at the right time. Essentially, you're developing a map to transform customers from browsers to believers, and from believers to buyers.

The Question is the Answer

You'll need to gather with anyone who "faces" customers daily. Ask them lots of questions to learn the answers that help define the Customer Journey Map:

- What questions do customers have at this stage of their journey?
- What content assets/information does the customer read or engage with?

- What opportunities exist to improve or enhance that engagement?
- How can we influence how the person feels, thinks, decides and acts?
- What new questions does a customer ask in the next stage of their journey
- What motivates the customer to progress to the next phase?
- What "changes" from stage to stage?

Chapter 1:
Content Planning

Content Planning

Content Planning Overview

Content planning pinpoints the opportunities, challenges and goals for content marketing success. Planning begins with a comprehensive analysis of the business, customers and competition. It includes SEO performance analysis, keyword research, editorial calendar, content category maps, social media "conversation" analysis, and customer journey and persona development.

The Content Plan: A GPS for Success

Content strategists often start the content marketing workflow by developing a content plan that asks and answers lots of questions. The amount of time that goes into this first step can vary from 10 to 400 hours, depending on the goals, budget, internal infrastructure and staff, resources and other factors.

Content plans are like a GPS for content marketing, defining the goals, strategy and tactics for success. Without a content plan, companies are shooting from the hip, blindly hoping for the highest return on investment.

Content Plans Answer These 6 Questions:

1. What are your content marketing goals?
2. Who is the target audience?
3. What content format will best connect with readers?
4. What is the content's purpose?
5. Where should you publish and promote the content?
6. What, exactly, will the performance boost be from the investment?

The answers to these six questions shape the vision and define the execution path for content marketing, summarized in what is called the content plan. As you move through this section, you'll see why these questions are important, and you'll get tips and hacks to answer them for your company or client. Some are more difficult to answer than others, but you'll learn how to find all the answers, even if you have a shoestring budget.

You'll also be able to calculate the answer to the last question, namely, how to measure and track the impact of your investments in content marketing. You'll sort out how to craft the best strategy within the constraints of your budget, resources and infrastructure. The good news is that lack of knowledge and know-how will no longer be a barrier to success. So hang on tight, take notes that will help you retain the information better (a proven fact), and enjoy the ride.

1. What are your content marketing goals?

There are many goals for content marketing and just as many methods to track performance. Companies "want it all" when it comes to content marketing performance, but focusing on just a few KPIs (Key Performance Indicators) is necessary if you are to drive strategy and develop tactics to achieve those goals. Consider just a few of the key metrics we'll be discussing later on in the performance chapter:

- **Time on Page** (Engaging content holds readers with a stickiness that can be measured.)
- **Shares** (Interesting content gets shared organically; with paid support (ppc), your "best content" can improve share.)
- **User Acquisition Cost** (Increasing spend for content investment should increase organic traffic and decrease user acquisition cost.)
- **Attribution of Content Investment** (Tracking the impact of a single content asset or group of assets.)
- **Sales** (Sales increases can be tied to increases in organic traffic and acquisition of customers in new marketing channels supported by content marketing.)
- **Leads** (The quality, as well as the volume, of leads can increase through investment in content assets for various stages of the customer journey.)
- **Lead Cost** (Total marketing spend/number of leads can improve with content investment and decreased investments in other non-performing channels.)
- **Churn** (Improving conversion rates of trials and/or improved customer retention is another tie-in.)
- **Lifetime Value** (Content asset investment supporting the customer service team should improve NPS [See Chapter 5 for an in-depth discussion of Net Promoter Score.] scores and customer satisfaction.)
- **Revenue** (More traffic, more leads, improved lifetime value and other positive indicators can be directly attributed to content marketing investment.)

These are just a few of the metrics that content can affect at any business. Not surprisingly, you'll need more than just content marketing to move the needle significantly with any of these benchmarks. Your products/services, people and processes all need to get on the same page and work together to achieve your goals. More on that later.

2. Who is the target audience?

One of the most crucial parts of the content plan is defining and describing the target audience. This involves a detailed study of the demographics and psychographics of the prospects and customers that drive revenue and sales. Deeply understanding your target audience helps you make decisions about subject matter, tone, language, style and word count. Developing customer personas is the starting point for many marketers.

Content Strategy MasterClass Resource Appendix:
Access several buyer personas and development resources, including a HubSpot template and samples by WriterAccess.

3. What content format will best connect with readers?

The content marketer has many types of assets from which to choose. These include articles, books and e-books, blog posts, case studies, guides, press releases, videos, webpages and white papers. Companies often start the content marketing workflow by randomly selecting particular content assets that they hope will appeal to readers. As noted before, this is a bad idea.

Instead, content strategists need to get under the skin of the target audience by listening to their needs, understanding their pain points in the buyers' journey and then researching the competitive landscape to determine the types of content assets that might resonate well with readers, solve their problems and connect with them in mysterious ways.

Learning about publishing frequency, quality, shares, channels and other competitive factors is one key to crafting the best strategy. Combine these findings with data analysis to determine what kind of content assets you need to deliver on your goals. Even a small amount of research can go a long way in strategy development. Remember that the more research you do, the more accurate will be the prediction of your return on investment.

 Content Strategy MasterClass Resource Appendix: Access a webinar with guest Kevin Donlin called Marketing Multipliers: 7 Ways to Sell without Selling in the Content Strategy MasterClass Resource Appendix.

4. What is the content's purpose?

Defining the purpose of the content and the action you want readers to take is an art and a science. For each content asset you create, you'll want to define its purpose beforehand. All your content assets also will need to tie into the customer journey. Each asset must relate to how the customer thinks and feels at the touch points throughout the journey. More on the customer journey later.

Here are just a few of the options to consider:

- Increase Awareness
- Educate and Enlighten
- Offer Surprise and Delight
- Be Relevant
- Empathize
- Enhance Meaningful Connection
- Align With Core Values
- Be Personal

The key is to be selective when choosing options and to be clear about your purpose. Trying to do too much with your content will make it difficult for writers (and content strategists) to achieve goals.

 Content Strategy MasterClass Resource Appendix: Link to Content Rules: How to Create Killer Blogs, Podcasts, Videos, E-books, Webinars That Engage Customers and Ignite Your Business by Ann Handley.

5. Where should we publish and promote our content?

The answer to this question is: Where do your readers, customers, prospects and fans go to find the information they want and need? To appeal and connect with readers, content strategists develop content with a tone and style appropriate for each channel. Technology, combined with testing, helps to find what works and what does not work.

One way to test the viability of a channel for future investments is to promote your best content on it. For example, take your best blog post or downloadable content asset, and "amplify" your visibility by running ads on Facebook and directing your current customers to them. Take a look at the views and engagement, conversions, upsells or revenue from any and all engaged customers.

At WriterAccess, we track social media engagement for each asset. When a post is generating a higher rate of likes, comments or shares, we boost the post with paid advertising to amplify the impact and reach new readers.

6. What, exactly, will the ROI be for the proposed investment?

Achieving content performance is one of the most challenging steps and is a universal pain point for content marketers. There are numerous tools to measure the impact of your content marketing. Content strategists create reports to track listing positions, traffic, user acquisition cost and conversion rates, and other relevant metrics.

Given that we have an entire section devoted to content performance, let's move on to other tips and advice for content planning.

Content Planning Tools

Curation	Performance	Research	Planning

To create a content plan, you'll need to arm yourself with some powerful research tools to harvest the information, insights and data you need to make the planning process work. Here are some suggestions for the right tools to use for those on a smaller budget.

TOP CURATION TOOLS

Google Alerts

Curata

Uberflip

TOP PERFORMANCE TOOLS

Google Analytics

ScribbleLive

TrackMaven

TOP RESEARCH TOOLS

Moz

RavenTools

SpyFu

TOP PLANNING TOOLS

Asana

DivvyHQ

WriterAccess Content Planner

Where to Begin: Scope of Project

Before you actually start the research for your content plan, it's wise to define the scope of the project, including the goals, process for adherence, proposed budget, deliverables and timeline. If you're hiring an outside agency to create a content plan, it will typically develop a Scope of Project that helps to set expectations and get everyone on the same page with respect to roles and goals for content marketing success.

Content Strategy MasterClass Resource Appendix:
Download sample proposals we developed for prospect customers when we were a full-service content marketing agency.

Competitive Research

Using some super-simple research tools, you can quickly compare how your website stacks up against the competition to determine the challenges and opportunities for content marketing. We suggest you home in on a few of the following factors as primary drivers, depending on the project scope.

	Your Website	Competitor 1	Competitor 2
Traffic Volume	●	●	●
PPC Spend	●	●	●
Content Portfolio	●	●	●
Content Authority	●	●	●
Publishing Frequency	●	●	●
Social Reach	●	●	●
Social Conversations	●	●	●
Testimonials	●	●	●
Partnerships	●	●	●
Internal Links	●	●	●
Inbound Links	●	●	●
SEO Strength	●	●	●
SEO Performance	●	●	●
Testing Practice	●	●	●

Pro Tip: Use SpyFu to quickly see how your website stacks up against the competition for much of the data above. Your answers will begin to reveal how hard it will be to capture market share and mind share in the search engines. Visit SpyFu.com

Customer Personas

Once the customer journey has been documented (previous chapter exercise), it should be pretty easy to develop customer personas based on what you have learned. This moves you from a focus on touch points and pain points to character development that everyone can relate to and keep in mind when creating content.

The answers to the following questions should be added to demographic and psychographic criteria for each of the buyer personas that you develop:

What is the name of the person and their background?
What are their particular wants and needs?
What habits and tendencies do they have?
What motivates them to take action?

 Content Strategy MasterClass Resource Appendix:
Download a Customer Persona we developed for WriterAccess.

Customer Storyboards

 Awareness **Consideration** **Purchase** **Experience** **Referral**

Storyboards are an excellent way to map out the customer journey visually, crystalizing exactly what customers are thinking or feeling as they migrate through the customer journey. If you have access to an empathetic illustrator and copywriter, they can create storyboards that help us "feel" what customers are thinking as they interact with the brand. Storyboarding also helps the content strategist emotionally connect with customers through facial expressions and headlines that define what they are "thinking," as if a story is unfolding. Do give storyboarding a try if you're looking to dive deeply into content marketing.

Content Assets

Articles   Books   Blogs   Studies   Guides

It is only AFTER you are armed with a deep understanding of the customer journey, keyword targets (coming in a few chapters), and competitive intelligence about how you stack up versus the competition, all rolled into a content plan, that you finally will be in a position to start making recommendations about the types of content assets you'll want to recommend to achieve your content marketing goals. Here's a partial list of the content assets you'll need to consider that might engage customers at different stages of the journey, and deliver on content marketing goals:

Articles	Press Releases
Books/e-Books	PPC Landing Pages
Blog Posts	Special Landing Pages
Case Studies	Videos
Informational Guides	Webinars
Podcasts	White Papers
Product/Service Guides	Workbooks (like this one)

Your role as a content strategist in this planning stage is to find the right content assets to put in front of the right readers at the right time. You'll see in a few minutes that the sample content plan does just that, with lots of science built in.

Publishing Frequency and the Editorial Calendar

I've probably stating the following line about 100 times when discussing content marketing: Forward-thinking companies are starting to think like old school publishers — gathering ideas, developing stories and publishing a steady stream of content that engages readers and keeps them coming back for more. **As it turns out, publishing content consistently** confirms to both the search engines and your readers that you care about delivering information, insights and inspiration that everyone wants and needs on a regular basis. But creating all this content can be challenging. Launching an editorial calendar will help you map out a visual plan to keep the content flowing and goals on track.

 __WriterAccess My Tools:__ Explore the link to a Content Planner and editorial calendar.

Link Building

You'll also need to build a link-building process into your content plan. The fastest and easiest way to build link popularity is within your own website. Cross-pollinating the content on your website by adding links to and from key pages is of prime importance. Doing so will guide readers and search engines to related content they might find interesting and helpful. Internal linking also helps search engine spiders with contextual relevancy, one of many key factors of search rankings these days. However, avoid "overlinking" your content; general best practice suggests that one or two links per page within your content is the optimal number. Let contextual relevancy and the potential for customer distraction be the factors that guide your choices.

Paid Advertising

Close analysis of your Google Analytics account will help pinpoint the pages on your website that drive the most traffic, conversion and sales. Once you discover those pages, you'll want to consider promoting that content with paid advertising to "amplify" the return on investment. The best content to amplify, and arguably the only content to amplify, is informative content packed with keen insights, counter-intuitive observations and authoritative advice that is FAR removed from any sales pitch.

Your content plan should feature a paid advertising amplification section. We'll cover this in much more detail in the Content Distribution chapter ahead.

Planning for Performance

As part of the planning process, you'll need to select a few KPIs that become the drivers for content strategy. We'll cover content performance in a future chapter, but for now it's pretty important that your content plan focuses on just a few tips that get everyone on your team vested in the KPIs you select.

 Pro Tip: Publish KPIs publicly every day to help drive performance and achieve goals.

In a Nutshell

Open your WriterAccess MasterClass account. Download and read through these two very different content plans, and study how the plans answer questions and pinpoint goals and guidelines for content marketing. Then dive into the Buyer Persona Builder at WriterAccess featured under My Tools and Planning. You're exercise is to create several Buyer Personas for your business or a client's business, saving it so it's ready to review and use for future orders, specifying for a writer which "persona" the content will be created for to help writers better understand the target audience.

Exercise

Follow these steps to create your own Buyer Personas using the WriterAccess Tools.

1. Download Sample Buyer Personas
2. Create Your Own Buyer Personas
    *   Visit My Tools at WriterAccess
    *   Click on Planner: Persona Builder
    *   Create Your Buyer Personas and Save

Certification Test

Then take the online Content Planning Test

About The Content Plans

The Magic Mountain plan took about 400 hours to complete, and the WriterAccess plan took about 80 hours. The Magic Mountain Content Plan was developed for a larger
company with a content marketing budget exceeding $500,000 per year. The smaller plan was developed for WriterAccess a few years ago; it works with a smaller budget of about $50,000 per year on content spend alone (not including the price to develop the content plan itself).

Smaller content marketing budgets do not necessarily have smaller impacts on the bottom line. It's all about the research that drives the strategy and finding the small victories that can deliver big results. Both content plans offer the methodology and strategy to achieve specific goals and gain significant competitive advantage in the marketplace. More importantly, they set expectations and become a blueprint for content marketing that can be measured weekly and monthly against goals and performance.

In both plans, the content strategist began the process by developing a Keyword Map using SpyFu to find the keywords driving organic traffic to all of the competitive websites, which was accomplished in just a few minutes. That raw data was then culled to eliminate duplicates, misspelled words and phrases that would be impractical for developing content.

All the raw data was hand-reviewed for each keyword, including current listing position for each of the competitors' websites and the client website, along with search volume and PPC price.
A final list of keywords worthy of targeting, called the Keyword Universe, was hand-selected and grouped into Keyword Silos that

aligned with topics for content. The content strategists then verified all these keywords were worthy of targeting for content creation and search engine optimization. The decision tree included lots of variables, including the company's current listing positions, difficulty of gaining listing positions, and the estimated spend for content and content marketing to achieve performance goals.

Another big part of the development of both of these content plans was the competitive research. Each competitor's content was hand reviewed
on its website, including the quantity and frequency of
content published. This data became critical to answer the question: How MUCH content do we need to capture organic market share?

Delivery of a content plan is the first step in developing and executing a content marketing strategy. But the content planning process will continually refine itself based on reader interests, ongoing performance and discovery of what resonates well with readers, customers and fans. Read through the plans to get a sense for what needs to be done to develop a content plan for your own company. Look for a few questions from the plans on your test for this chapter.

Chapter 2:
Content Creation

Content Creation

Content Creation Overview

Are you ready to start creating content that appeals to both readers and search engines? At this step, you leverage content plans, SEO insights and editorial calendars to develop timely, relevant, useful content that will connect with your target audience.

Here are a few questions you will learn to answer:

> What's the best tone, style and voice for my content?
> How do I develop that voice?
> What are examples of amazing content that hits the mark?
> Where do I find new writers?
> How do I onboard new writers to the goals?
> What content engages my readers?
> How do I create content for different channels?

Creating Great Content: Snap, Crackle and Pop

As it turns out, content marketing is more about the content than it is about marketing. This section focuses on the process of creating content. But not just any content, great content. The world doesn't need more mediocre content. Your customers certainly don't need more mediocre content.

All that sounds terrific, but creating a steady stream of great content is challenging. First, we need to define it; then we need to explain how to create it.

What Is Great Content?

Great content is one step beyond the ordinary. It fulfills most of the marketing goals you'll ever have. It targets specific readers and hooks them with information they want and need. It engages them with copy well written and stories well told by writers with the skills and expertise to transform "good" into "great." Passion about the topic certainly plays a big role in creating great content. But the structure of great content itself seems to be the key. This is something I call "snap, crackle and pop" — the key elements of great content.

 Content Strategy MasterClass Resource Appendix: For your viewing pleasure, check out an animated video I put together called Snap, Crackle and Pop.

Snap

The first of the three key elements of great content is "snap." Content snaps when a headline or title stops the reader and inspires him or her to dive in and read on. Here are some approaches for headlines that snap:

- Write a line that promises to deliver helpful advice.
- Evoke emotion by telling readers how they can achieve pleasure or avoid pain.
- Ask a relevant question.
- Offer a list of "do's" or "don'ts."
- Use a number to indicate your content has a list.
- Hook readers with an inspiring idea that speaks to a desire.
- Address a pressing problem or pain that causes frustration.
- Demonstrate you understand and care about your readers.
- Promise success with a specific favorable outcome.

 Content Strategy MasterClass Resource Appendix: Link to a tool by CoSchedule that rates your headline SEO value and potential to generate social shares and traffic.

Crackle

Great content also has elements of what I call "crackle." Content crackles when it touches the heart, makes a reader smile, and/or releases a rush of dopamine to the brain. For years, medical researchers believed that only drugs were engaging to the point of addiction. Neuroimaging changed all that in the last 15 years, confirming that many things, even stories, for example, can be addicting. To succeed with your content, you need to enhance the "rush" readers experience as they take in great stories, well told. (See reference below.) Content with crackle turns good into great by promoting familiarity, loyalty and other elements that bind readers to your story, and your brand.

Some effective ways to elevate crackle include:

- Unleashing a story
- Stirring up controversy
- Surprising people
- Stating strong opinions
- Involving readers' emotional triggers
- Offering rewards for participation

Pop

And, finally, great content pops when it motivates a reader, viewer or listener to take action that is measurable. Content with pop invites and delivers engagement. It moves readers to reply, comment, download, like, share the content or buy.

Inserting a call to action is a common practice to help achieve this goal. Pop refers to the desirable action or goals for the content, and it varies from stage to stage of the customer journey:

- At the top of the funnel, pop transforms browsers to believers with content the readers can get behind, believe in and share.

- In the middle of the funnel, pop inspires action that reflects deeper interest. It could be attending a webinar, asking for a consultation, taking a product demo, signing up for a trial, completing a questionnaire, or other actions.
- The ultimate pop is a conversion at the middle of the funnel or a referral to another customer at the end of the funnel, which starts the customer journey through snap, crackle and pop all over again.

Great content has snap, crackle and pop throughout the customer journey.

Great Content Gets Shared

Content that snaps, crackles and pops is not only consumed — because it resonates with its audience — but shared via the many social channels consumers now rely on. As a result, the conversion potential of your content can be dramatically magnified. Here are a few amazing tools that instantly reveal the most-shared content for any website, topic, search term or even author:

Pro Tool: BuzzSumo is a search tool that tracks content on all social networking sites and ranks them based on the number of shares on Facebook, Twitter, LinkedIn, Google+ and Pinterest. Use BuzzSumo to identify content that works well and to learn which topics garner the most attention. Then, reverse-engineer the elements of this content and apply the techniques to your own material. Trust me, this is something that all great content creators do regularly. Observe what works and what does not work in the social sphere, and apply what you've learned.

The Eight Ingredients of Great Content

Barry Feldman points out that the best content contains the following ingredients:

	Daily Value
SERVING SIZE	1
Purpose	100%
Value	**100%**
Relevance	100%
Timeliness	**100%**
Emotion	100%
Novelty	**100%**
Simplicity	100%
Credibility	**100%**

Feldman points out that the best chefs use the highest quality organic ingredients sourced by local farmers in their communities and around the world. Great content creators do the same thing. They use the best elements in their stories, even sourcing other experts and content assets to cross-pollinate and build authority. He has identified eight key ingredients of great content. Let's talk about why they're important. But remember, as I've pointed out to Barry a few times, it's not the ingredients alone that make the cake taste great; it's how you bake the cake. More on that later.

1. Purpose

Great content has purpose that's clear. It gives the audience something memorable to dig into, think about, relate to and engage with in mysterious ways. Defining purpose is not only a tactic for many writers; it's the starting point for greatness.

Marketing itself tends to have a single purpose: to drive profitable customer action and revenue goals. That single-minded focus can cause marketers to lose sight of the many intermediate purposes that can take place at stages along the customer journey. A consideration of that journey requires rethinking the element of purpose.

To measure whether your purpose has been achieved, you'll need to establish key performance indicators (KPIs) that align with the goal. Remember that purpose is not necessarily conversion or the sale. From our deeper understanding of the customer journey, purpose may take on many forms, such as connecting, understanding, gaining insight or mitigating fear.

 Pro Tip: Don't confuse purpose with KPIs. For example, great storytellers want to captivate their audiences. You won't find "audience captivation" on any marketing KPI list. But you will find that every TED Talks speaker understands the art of telling stories with purpose that captivates the audience and then, and only then, triggers all the shares.

2. Value

Great content delivers value by ameliorating the readers' pain and/or helping to bring them pleasure. It enhances the life of your reader, at work, at play or in some way. As it turns out, creating value is pretty easy to do. Socratic techniques come in handy here. Asking questions leads to the answers you need to know to make marketing work well.

 Exercise: Finding Value Using Socratic Techniques
  • Develop a list of questions you'd like to ask readers at each stage of the customer journey.

  • Map the pain points you learn about to the content you publish.

  • Think beyond your products and services; ask thoughtful questions to find rich answers.

  • Based on the answers, create content that aligns with the value your readers demand.

3. Relevance

Value is rooted in relevance. To create relevant content, you have to develop a deep empathy for your reader. Creators of great content develop content that speaks to buyers on a personal level, in a style that connects with them at their exact stage of the customer journey.

Tricks of the Trade to Being Relevant

- Localize your content.
- Personalize your content.
- Empathize with your readers.
- Familiarize yourself with what works and what does not work.

 Pro Tip: I'm sure you've heard of the sales technique to talk at the same pace as your customer on the phone. Bottom line, it works. Customers want to buy from people who are like them. The same is true with content creation. Take a look at how your clients create content, including looking over their email communications and/or blog posts to learn about their style. Document the examples in the Personas or Storyboards, using their actual words to help future writers learn how they write and think.

4. Timeliness

You've likely heard the distinction between fresh content — breaking news — and evergreen content — always relevant. What you may not have heard is that most traffic to websites stems from content that is well beyond the fresh stage. While most social media posts are usually fresh, much is not actually breaking news. But it is often fresh in the eyes of readers, who then share it with their own readers and fans.

Great content can be timely or evergreen. It's important to create a mix of both, depending on your industry, and to have the flexibility to adjust your publishing schedule to include important new developments.

Pro Tip: If your content is somewhere between fresh and evergreen, it's likely to be old news, easily passed over and never shared. Such content is very far from great.

5. Emotion

"The future belongs to those who can make emotional connections in the market. We are in the game now of creating loyalty beyond price, beyond attribution, beyond benefit, beyond product, beyond form, beyond process, beyond technology."

— Former Saatchi & Saatchi CEO Kevin Roberts

Roberts said marketing must include a good story that contains emotion and humor. The idea is to inform but at the same time entertain.

Neuromarketing, a relatively new science that has surfaced only in the last 10 years, helps us understand the new rules of decision-making that affect design and content creation. Don't make the mistake of believing readers rely on reasoning to make decisions; neuromarketing has taught us that it's what we feel that drives our choices.

Neuromarketing pioneer Douglas Van Praet, author of "Unconscious Branding," explains the emotional connection that content creators make with their audience. He notes that content that connects with readers contains the element of story that is essential for engagement.

Actor Kevin Spacey joins the content marketing revolution with his contention that the stories that we tell should awaken emotions with surprise, amazement, curiosity and uncertainty. Craft your content with these emotions in mind, and you'll increase your chances of attracting and engaging an audience.

 Content Strategy MasterClass Resource Appendix: Links to reference books on the neuromarketing and neuroscience topic.

6. Novelty

Look up the word "novel," and you'll see it's an adjective meaning "new or unusual in an interesting way." Readers of this workbook have their own stories about the impact of novelty in their lives. In content marketing, novelty means striving to offer something that hasn't been seen before. Content marketers deliver novelty for many reasons: It piques readers' interest, makes them curious, gets them engaged. Try to include a healthy dose of novelty in your content.

 Exercise: Read your latest content asset that you think offers something new or unusual. Now speak with someone who has read that content to see if he or she agrees with your conclusion. Are you in tune with your audience's level of knowledge? Put your novelty to the test.

7. Simplicity

You've probably heard the KISS principle: "Keep It Simple, Stupid." Here's some fresh insight we should all be aware of: Writing is rewriting. Only then can you find true simplicity.

Great content conveys its meaning as simply as possible. This is even more important now that we're reading more content online. A CMO Council study, "Better Lead Yield in the Content Marketing Field," ranked "ease of access, understanding and readability" as the second-most valued characteristic of online content.

Many content marketers fail the "ease" test. And many do so unwittingly, by not recognizing that the online reading experience differs from reading words on paper. On paper — that is, in books, newspapers, magazines and mail — readers are willing to tolerate pages densely populated with copy. Online, they aren't. Compose your pages with this in mind and cater to the skimmer:

- Write shorter passages.

- Use more white space and add more line breaks.
- Use ample visual cues.
- Add images and captions.
- Set key points apart to break the monotony.
- Include subheads generously.
- Create lists.

 Content Strategy MasterClass Resource Appendix: Link to the reference CMO Council study and ease of access test.

8. Credibility

Great content is 100 percent credible. When marketers misinterpret, re-use, misuse, and abuse statistics and quotations to support their positions, credibility vanishes in an instant, and often forever. So take care to back up the points you make with research, facts and quotations that you can document or link to the original source. To provide the highest quality content, you should use only sources that you personally believe to be authoritative. Your reputation as a credible content creator is based in large part on whom you quote, whom you reference, whom you choose to allow into your content. Do share sources with readers; it's the right thing to do. There's great content to be found from universities, government agencies, trade associations, research studies, best-selling authors — heck, even from friends!

How We Create Great Content: Style, Storytelling and Visuals

There are four important processes for creating great content:

1. Tone and Style
2. Style Flexing
3. Storytelling
4. Visual Elements

Tone and Style

Many companies develop style guides that establish standards for both the writing and design of all content assets created for the brand. These standards may be included in the creative brief or be part of a separate style guide. Shown here is an editorial style guide that covers:

- Use of the AP Stylebook for grammar and punctuation issues
- Content tone and style
- Educational/promotional balance
- Topic suggestions

 Content Strategy MasterClass Resource Appendix:
Download a sample Writing Style Guide, Brand Guide and Creative Brief that help get writers, designers and other creative team members on the same page.

Style Flexing

As mentioned above, you improve your chances to "connect" with your audience by matching the writing style to the type of content asset and the typical tone and style that readers expect. A long-form blog post that dives deeply into a complex topic and a 150-word email are trying to accomplish distinct goals and will require distinctly different writing approaches. When you hire or assess writers for your projects, look for their ability to "style flex" for different asset types and target audiences. Writers with style flex can adjust their style to:

- Compose content that addresses a variety of goals.
- Speak to different target audiences or personas with copy that will resonate.
- Apply the ingredients that work best for the project at hand.
- Convey the brand personality.

Flexible writers will often analyze existing writing samples from a client's portfolio that proved effective and adjust their style accordingly.

You may be able to find experienced writers with the ability to adapt their style. However, if your content presents a complex list of requirements, you may prefer to build an expanded team of writers that includes those who specialize in certain industries, media types and/or writing styles.

Writing Style Contest

Let's face it: The writing style coveted by a customer can be fairly subjective and not always easy to articulate to writers. One way to pinpoint the best writing style for a brand is to host a writing style contest with a few different writers to compare and contrast different tones and styles. Here's how it works at WriterAccess:

- Select three different writers who meet your skill, experience and price requirements.
- Launch a Writing Style Contest using our special order form.
- Create one "order" for content that details your specifications and goals.
- Place the same order to all three writers.
- Offer feedback to each of them, after review of the first draft.
- Take a look at the final drafts, and compare the style and tone used by each writer.
- Pick the winning style that best aligns with your brand.
- Work with the writer on projects that need that style and tone.

Storytelling

As noted in the introduction, there is quite a bit of science behind why stories are so powerful and important to our communication. As a content strategist, part of your role is to find and tell your clients' stories in the best way possible. Great stories take readers on an emotional journey, and they're typically remembered long after the tale is over. A great story might be touching, scary, funny, shocking, sad, inspiring or maybe just strange, counterintuitive or unpredictable. Great stories include:

- An emotional, personal journey.
- Time and place or some form of context.
- Interesting characters the reader can relate to.
- Conflict: something or someone stands in the way of the protagonist's journey.
- A series of plot developments.
- Suspense... What happens next?
- Surprise, delight, shock, warmth, love or any type of emotional trigger.
- Resolution, which is sometimes a lesson learned.

 Content Strategy MasterClass Resource Appendix: Link to Content Strategist Barry Feldman's blog post covering the core elements of storytelling.

Visual Elements

Data makes a strong case that using visuals is essential in producing content that engages customers:

- We currently spend between 8.5 and 9 hours per day on screens, including online, mobile and TV. (The New York Times and Huffington Post)
- About 90 percent of the information absorbed by the brain is visual and is processed 60,000X faster than text. (3M and Zabisco)
- Research confirms that use of images with content increases engagement by as much as 94 percent. (Getty Images)

Tips for Better Visuals

- Choose your stock images wisely for originality and alignment with your brand.
- Tap into AB/multivariate testing to find out which images and videos inspire and perform.
- Get inspired by graphic artists who transform ideas into campaigns that motivate and drive business growth.

Here are a few resources for stock images that can tell and augment the story:

123RF	Dreamstime	Graphic Stock
BigStock	Fotolia	iStock
Corbis Images	Getty Images	ShutterStock
		Veer

Video

Video is another essential ingredient of great content. Our brains are hardwired to tune in closely to the human face for information. Eye contact enhances believability. Body language conveys emotion, which increases appeal. The human voice is perceived as highly meaningful. And movement grabs attention. Further building the case for adding video to your marketing mix are the following data:

- Online browsers are 85 percent more likely to buy a product or service after watching a video. (Internet Retailer)
- 70 percent of marketers claim that video is superior to other content types in conversion. (Demand Metric)
- Video on landing pages can increase conversions by 80 percent. (Unbounce)
- The average user sees 32.3 videos a month. (comScore)
- YouTube is the third-most-trafficked website and home to the second-largest search engine.

Content Strategy MasterClass Resource Appendix:
Explore links to resources like Dissolve, Pond5, RevoStock, ClipCanvas, Footage.net, VideoHive, Videvo, Video Blocks, Stock Footage and more. Also explore a five-minute video of author Dr. Susan Weinschenk explaining the four reasons why video is so compelling and persuasive.

The Content Creators: Nine Characteristics of Great Writers

Hundreds of thousands of writers, designers, illustrators and other creative talents are now only a click away, available through the many online platforms that connect companies and freelancers. Many of these platforms monitor the quality of the work and level of service, enabling you to find proven talent. Let's explore the nine characteristics of great writers to help you pinpoint the best of the best.

1. Freakishly Passionate About the Topic

You can just tell when a writer is passionate about a topic. The word selection is more sophisticated, the writing tone is stronger, and the style is more confident. Somehow, we read between the lines and connect with the author in strange and mysterious ways. Passion is likely the driver of this connection. Look for writers with deep experience in industries and topics. They'll have a passion for the topic that keeps them up at night, trying to find what's new and what's next.

2. Mastery of Digital Media

Great content writers are totally in tune with how readers consume digital media. They're sensitive to the idea that the reader:

- Is forever in search of specific things and wants to find answers fast.

- Wants up-to-date, relevant, straightforward information.
- Craves advice from authorities.
- Is looking out for number one — wants information of benefit to himself or herself.

Look for writers who are aware of trends in digital marketing, read content marketing publications and blogs, and are on top of the latest technology and tools. Test prospective writers to gauge their grasp of the needs of mobile, internet-savvy readers.

3. Understand the Paradox of Choice

Most of us assume that more choices will produce better options and greater satisfaction, when, in fact, the greater our choices, the less happy we tend to be. Great writers are sensitive to the paradox of choice; they understand the stress and anxiety that the expansion of choice causes consumers. Look for writers who:

- Know how to discover the rules for decision-making.
- Develop decision-making maps and processes.
- Create methodologies for buying decisions.
- Forge simplicity into the decision-making process.

 Content Strategy MasterClass Resource Appendix: Reference to Barry Schwartz's book "The Paradox of Choice: Why Less is More" revealing that reducing consumer choices can greatly reduce anxiety for shoppers.

4. Appeal to Different Readers

Great content writers can speak the language of the readers they aim to engage. These chameleons of style can toggle smoothly between such extremes as "Impulsive Andy," the quick-to-buy consumer, and "Sophisticated Sally," the rational consumer who wants to go deep before she buys.

Great writers understand that many readers want detailed information and they deliver it. They also understand that another sector of the audience is impulsive and wants a leaner form of content upon which to make buying decisions. Look for writers with the ability to create content for each type of consumer, or for the buyer personas you develop for your brand voice.

5. Know How to Shape Perception

Great writers can touch readers in important ways with stories that shape perception. Such storytellers are hard to find because perceptive stories are harder to develop. Look for writers who understand how to craft great stories that shape perception. Some of the perceptions that these writers can guide are:

- What's worth living for?
- What's worth dying for?
- What's worth buying?
- What's worth upgrading?
- Why should I take action?

 Content Strategy MasterClass Resource Appendix:
Reference to Robert McKee's book "Story: Substance, Structure, Style and the Principles of Screenwriting" explaining how great writers are adept at shaping perceptions.

6. Know How to Find New Meaning

Great writers know how to find new value in products and services without overtly selling those products or services. Their writing helps readers better understand solutions and how to solve problems with ease. The work they create delivers value, insight and wisdom.

Look for writers who show curiosity — the driver for discovering meaning. Journalists are typically strong in this area, well-versed in finding the story by probing for answers with lots and lots of questions.

7. Understand the Power of Storytelling

Selling readers on the features and benefits of your products and services will not achieve your marketing goals. Readers simply are not receptive to being sold to these days. Thus, the best writers use storytelling skills to transform browsers to buyers. Look for writers who can transform traditional "selling" scripts into storytelling magic that delivers every time.

- **Preliminary:** First impressions and headline architecture **>>**
  You're confused. But you're not alone.
- **Investigating:** Knowledge-seeking and trust-building **>>**
  You'd be surprised to see who's using this product. We were.
- **Demonstrating Capability:** How products solve problems **>>**
  Let's say you were having trouble with X. But suddenly…
- **Obtain Permission:** Drive action, sign up, download or buy **>>**
  We'd like for you to give us a try. And we're so convinced you'll…

8. Take Creative Risks

Great writers aren't afraid to take risks to bring a concept to life, engage the reader and make a point memorable. A risk can pay off when it:

- Makes teeth chatter.
- Makes people talk.
- Makes people laugh.
- Touches the heart.
- Creates buzz.

Look for writers who take risks. Even better, find out when those risks paid off. But remember, to find winning campaigns and assets, writers likely stumble over lots of non-performers before they find the winners. Don't be afraid to encourage writers to take creative risks that may help achieve performance goals.

 Content Strategy MasterClass Resource Appendix: Reference to Bonnie Neubauer's book "The Write-Brain Workbook" highlighting how great writers take creative risks.

9. Sensational Style Flexors

Writing style is essentially the personality you express in your writing. Great writers understand how to "FLEX" their writing style to best connect with the audience and achieve goals. The context, media and reader experience are key factors in determining the best style for a project. A specific writing style might include choices about:

- Diction
- Punctuation use
- Headline and subhead placement
- Word choice
- Sentence and paragraph length
- Abstract vs. concrete imagery

It's crucial to establish a writing style for your content. Though a creative brief may touch on the subject, content strategists would do well to invest additional time in discussing style, exploring options and developing standards.

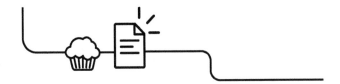

Baking the Content Marketing Cake: Content vs. Great Content

You've learned the ingredients of great content above, and you'll certainly want to use them. But when it comes to a cake, it's not only the ingredients that make it delectable. How you bake it can make all the difference in the world. The same is true in content marketing, where the "how" often receives short shrift.

Here's the problem with how we think about the content creation process:

1. Clients list all the requirements and specifications for a project, including a creative brief.
2. Clients offer examples of the tone and style that will resonate well with the audience.
3. Writers reverse-engineer the ingredients and elements that meet the requirement.
4. Writers artfully combine all the ingredients provided by the client.
5. Writers deliver the cake with all the ingredients, and it gets approved.

What's wrong with this process? We assume that when we artfully mix all the ingredients, the cake will taste great, and the content will be great. Instead, it's how we craft the content and tell the story that make the content great. Snap, crackle and pop are just a few of the elements. It's really up to the writer to craft style, tone and value proposition into great content that engages readers and drives performance.

Study the elements that separate great content from good content, inspired by Kevin Roberts in his book "Sissimo." You'll see a distinction between zestless content that creates restless readers, and zestful content that moves them forward.

📄 Content	📄 Great Content
Fills You Up	**Moves You On**
Facts	**Acts**
Citing	**Exciting**
Reams	**Dreams**
Promotional	**Emotional**
Static	**Dramatic**
Checklists	**Casts of Characters**
Compiling	**Compelling**
Annotated	**Animated**
Feeding the Brain	**Touching the Heart**
Expires	**Inspires**

 Content Strategy MasterClass Resource Appendix:
Reference to Kevin Roberts' book "Sissimo" exploring sight, sound, motion and emotion of great stories and great advertising spots.

Why Readers Share

Perhaps the ultimate measure of great content is its shareability. Great content gets passed around in the social sphere. Great writers understand why readers share. That becomes an important part of the content marketing, cake-baking process. The New York Times conducted a research project on sharing and discovered these surprising insights about why readers share:

- Bring value and entertainment to others.
- Define yourself to others with online persona(s).
- Grow and nourish relationships, especially online.
- Exhibit connection to the world and community.
- Showcase support for a brand or cause.

 Source: New York Times Customer Insight Group

Aligning Quality With Price

In general, when you pay more for writing services, you should expect higher quality and better performance for the content you buy. But you may still wonder: Exactly what elements of great writing should I expect when I pay more? That's where my second book comes in: "The Professional Writing Skill and Price Guide" walks you through the elements of what to expect when you pay more. By doing so, it creates a common set of expectations for both buyers and sellers of writing services.

 Content Strategy MasterClass Resource Appendix:
Download a copy of the "Professional Writing Skill and Price Guide".

Creating Great Content Is a Team Sport

In his classic book "Ogilvy on Advertising," David Ogilvy, one of the greatest marketing writers of his time, highlights the importance of building out a team that can deliver on its goals when it comes to marketing and advertising.

"If each of us hires people who are smaller than we are, we shall become a company of dwarfs. But if each of us hires people who are bigger than we are, we shall become a company of giants."

— David Ogilvy

The key in today's marketplace is not only to hire well, but to onboard your writers to your content marketing methodology, technology and strategy. We'll dive much deeper into building out content teams in the Content Management section of this workbook, so stay tuned.

CERTIFICATION REQUIREMENT:

In a Nutshell

Open your WriterAccess Tools and the Creative Brief Builder. Create and develop a creative brief for a particular writing project, documenting the tone, style, target audience, company background and goals for the project. You're creative brief will document information a writer needs to successfully complete the project outlined in the brief.

Exercise

Follow these steps to create a Creative Brief using the WriterAccess Tools.

1. Download Sample Creative Brief in the MasterClass
2. Create Your Own Creative Brief using the Creative Brief Builder
3. Save Your Creative Brief

Certification Test

Then take the online Content Creation Test

Creative Brief

In this section, you'll use our Creative Brief Wizard to develop a creative brief for a writing project you plan on creating sometime in the future. But before you take on that task, let's walk through a couple of key points to consider. A creative brief is the most beneficial method for summarizing and communicating all of the relevant information needed by any and all team members to create content that connects with your audience and achieves specific goals. It includes a concise summary of the key factors that will impact content creation, and it's meant to inspire original, exciting and creative copy that will engage readers and motivate them to return.

The Creative Brief: Who, What, When and Why

Fitting all the details into a single resource that defines the project parameters can be a challenging undertaking, depending on the size of the project. Typically, creative briefs are created for content asset types such as blog posts or bigger projects such as white papers. The brief often includes metrics and samples that help guide the writing process.

Developing the creative brief can be the responsibility of one or more team members:

- Content strategist
- Researchers
- Marketing manager
- Managing editor
- Business owner
- Creative director
- All of the above

Creative briefs help content strategists define:

- Brand information
- Target audience
- Tone of voice
- Writing style
- Specifications
- Requirements
- Goals and objectives

Let's take a look at what's included in a creative brief:

- Definition of the project and its scope
- Background information about the company, its brand and DNA
- Target audience, including demographics and psychographics
- Project objective and purpose
- Tone, voice and style elements
- Requirements for sources, quotations and links
- Things to be excluded or avoided
- Relevant samples to help guide the writer or creative team
- Sources that will be useful to reference and research
- Any other information that will help guide the writing, design and development of the content

Chapter 3:
Content Optimization

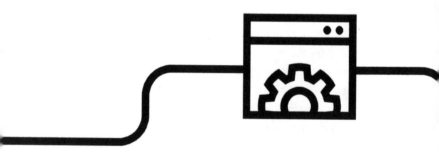

Content Optimization

Content Optimization Overview

Content optimization is the science of optimizing content for readers and search engines. Success depends on finding the important keywords and hot topics and scoring content for SEO strength. It also includes page optimization, content testing, directory submissions, link building, sitemap architecture and much more.

In this chapter, these are some of the questions you will answer:

What are best practices for landing page optimization?
How can I develop A/B tests to optimize conversions?
What are the secrets to optimizing content?
What's the latest with off-page and on-page link building?
What skills does a Search Optimization Specialist have?
What skills does a Pro Web Optimizer have?
What's next with Google and optimization?

Content Optimization

We tend to think of "content optimization" as the art and science of optimizing content for search engines, a practice designed to improve our ranking so that we can drive more organic traffic to our websites and improve market share and mind share with prospects and customers. In actuality, the scope of content optimization has grown considerably. In general, it is now all about getting the right content to the right people (and search bots) at the right time, helping to achieve specific goals for traffic growth, engagement, sharing and conversion rate improvements. That is both an art and a science. In this section, we'll explore three types of optimization:

I. Search Engine Optimization

A key role for content strategists is to advise clients on how to get content discovered via search, which is arguably the most important digital marketing channel. In this chapter, we'll run through the basics of SEO and show you how to boost SEO with topic and content optimization.

II. Landing Page Optimization

It's one thing to optimize content for search engines. It's a very different strategy to optimize landing pages for both readers and search engines. In this section, we'll discuss how to use keywords to improve the code, navigation and conversion on your web pages for better results.

III. Conversion Rate Optimization

And finally, we'll take a quick look at optimizing for conversion, using some material that explains how CROs, or "conversion rate optimizers," use testing to improve results.

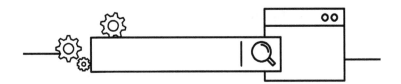

I. SEARCH ENGINE OPTIMIZATION

Search engines can be the largest driver of traffic to your website or blog. Optimizing your content and landing pages for search engines is a top priority. This includes the content on your social channels, email and any content published on the web. Well-optimized content will bring in not only new readers but also readers who have a greater intent to buy and a higher tendency to refer other readers and potential buyers to your website.

SEO Basics: Create the Most Relevant and Valuable Content

Far too many content strategists neglect optimization. They believe it's technical, hard to understand and time-consuming. By the end of this section, you'll learn that the master of search engine optimization is Google. Google advises you to create timely, relevant websites and pages that users want to use and share. The only way to "cheat" the system is to amplify your great content with paid promotion, to help start the sharing process that will eventually take over organically if the content is great.

 Content Strategy MasterClass Resource Appendix:
Reference to Barry Feldman article and book "SEO Simplified for Short Attention Spans" which demystifies the search engine optimization process.

The Search Engine Results Page (SERP)

Here's a search engine results page, a version of something you see on your screen multiple times every day. Professionals call the page a "SERP" for short. SERPs may appear quite different depending on the nature of the search. The search engine does its best to understand the context of your search, so results may include images, videos, news stories, maps or even quick answers to your inquiries, culled from authoritative sources. For instance, a search for "baseball scores" will indeed present the scores of recent games. A search for the definition of a word may show you the definition in the "knowledge graph." Generally speaking, however, SERPs feature three main elements:

Pay-per-click ads
Advertisers pay to present their ads via an auction-style bidding system. Google is the pioneer of this system, and its paid advertising program, Google AdWords, is by far the most well-known and used.

Organic listings
A large portion of the page lists up to 10 results that are not paid or sponsored. Organic results include a page title, a URL, and a description of the page or excerpt from it, which is often described as a "snippet."

Related search terms
At the bottom of a SERP, you will usually find a list of similar search terms, intended to help users dig deeper and find answers.

Why Are SERPs Important to Understand?

Search engine results are not links to websites. Instead, SERPs contain links to pages that have information that's relevant to your question. People use search engines because they want answers. Search engines serve up results based on many factors. The best answers may not always be on the first page, but the top listings on the first page get 90 percent of the clicks. To succeed with search engine optimization, you need to get your content on the first page of the search engine results. That's the goal.

What Gets Ranked on Page 1?

Search rankings are largely based on quality and authority. In years past, before Google made significant changes to its algorithm, quality and authority were judged to be one and the same. That is to say, the quality of the page was assessed mostly by its authority. At that time, links served as the primary indicator of both quality and authority. Unfortunately, this gave rise to a large number of black hat SEO businesses on the web. Those who liked to call themselves professional "SEOs" aimed to increase the authority of webpages by using any possible tactic to acquire links. In time, the link-based system failed. The major search engines themselves thankfully engineered it out of existence through consistent algorithm updates.

Today, while it's understood that search engines use hundreds of criteria to determine rankings, links have retained some popularity and remain a significant factor. The good news is that search engines are better able to make quality assessments based on factors besides backlinks. Content continues to be king, and social shares are more of a driving force for authority. Consequently, SERP results are getting better all the time.

Your Content Needs Relevance Indicators

If you're a modern, ambitious content strategist, in addition to written content, you're likely creating, curating and publishing images, video and audio-based content. Of that considerable content output, search engines recognize your words and not a lot more at the moment. Thus, the keywords you select will be the trigger for relevance to the search engine. But you need to select your words wisely, thinking well beyond their "popularity." Use popularity as a starting point, but use advanced tools to help you find relevant topics that will engage readers and keep them returning to your site.

Here's a quick exercise to help you take keyword research to the next level and apply that research to content strategy:

1. Go to SpyFu.com and drop in one of your top competitors' domain names to find 10 keywords that drive traffic to their website.
2. Go to AnswerThePublic.com and drop in those keywords or keyword phrases to learn common questions.
3. Go to BuzzSumo.com and do the same, searching for popular topics in the social sphere related to those keywords.

This exercise will help you shift the focus of SEO from keyword popularity to reader engagement with popular topics related to those keywords.

Search-Ranking Factors

The good news about search ranking is that it's no longer based entirely on links to your page. The bad news? Experts estimate there are now 200-plus search-ranking factors. You can't optimize for every one of them, but you don't have to. To make the right choices, though, it's helpful to understand, to the degree you can, what the factors are, which are most important, and what you can do to help your cause.

However, you should also understand that no known list of search-ranking factors exists. For proprietary reasons that should be obvious, Google will not publish its sacred list or reveal its algorithm. The absence of a definitive list has led to swarms of conjecture, speculation and misinformation flying around the web.

Two authorities on the topic are Searchmetrics and Moz, companies that dedicate significant resources to developing and testing related theories. The companies publish updates on their findings often — because the game changes often. Google updates its algorithm 300 to 500 times a year. In this course, we'll give Searchmetrics and Moz the authority they deserve, while at the same time we'll discuss search-ranking factors at a very basic level so you can proceed with some level of confidence. Even though these factors are closely guarded secrets, search engine results deliver useful clues to ranking them.

 Content Strategy MasterClass Resource Appendix:
Reference to a table of SEO success factors.

Factor 1: Link Popularity

At least for the time being, link popularity continues to be an important part of the algorithm that determines SERP. The two types of links are inbound and outbound. Inbound are links from other sites to your site. Outbound are from your site to another. The source of each of the inbound links and whether that source is viewed as a high-quality site are factors that Google weighs. Here are a couple of things you should know about link popularity:

- Link popularity helps to determine the authority or rank of a website.
- Not all links have the same value. Certain links to your website have more authority than others, based on their link popularity.
- Links from respected sites and contextually relevant sites seem to weigh more heavily in ranking.
- Linking to other trusted websites can positively influence ranking.
- Internal links within your own website can have a positive impact on ranking.

For decades, the importance of links has been well understood — perhaps too well understood. As a result, millions of website owners have blindly practiced reckless optimization techniques, such as buying links or creating websites for the single purpose of link building. These tactics are now called "black hat." If detected and confirmed, they can get the sites involved removed from SERPs.

Factor 2: Semantically Related Phrases

Content optimization demands that you understand semantic search. Semantic search uses semantics, or the science of meaning, rather than a list of loosely related links, to produce highly relevant search results. Semantic search involves understanding the searcher's intent and context. Take a look at these two sentences: "I had a big beef with my boss the other day" and "My steak was cooked to perfection." A search engine could interpret "big beef" as an argument, but the second sentence offers the context of "steak" to better classify the content. Search engines look for context as one of many methods to deliver the best results to knowledge seekers.

To address the challenge of semantic misinterpretation, use terms that are semantically related to the keywords you've selected to optimize your content. The best place to start is with common sense. Perform searches yourself and take a look at the results, particularly the words Google actually lists on the results page. Semantically related phrases will appear on the SERP when you search for a particular keyword. Dive into keyword research tools for suggestions on contextually relevant phrases to use for optimization. That will help make your case for top listings.

Semantic Search: Three Questions

OK, you have a topic in mind for content, and you're ready to begin the keyword research process. Here are three questions you'll need to answer to get your post or page on the first Google search page:

1. What keywords relate to my topic that I should target?
2. Do I have a chance to rank for them?
3. Can I make the best page on the web for this topic?

Let's scrutinize these questions to come up with the answers you need.

Question #1: What keywords relate to my topic that I should target?

This first question is surprisingly simple to answer. Just use the popular tool Google Keyword Planner. It's free, though you need to sign up for a Google AdWords account to gain access to it. The tool was created to serve the research needs of those planning to buy Google pay-per-click ads, but you can use it without making any purchases or commitments.

You can enter one or more keywords, or keyword phrases, that you are considering for your optimization efforts. The results will show search volume for those exact phrases and up to 800 suggestions deemed relevant by the Google algorithm. So you may have hundreds of alternate ideas to consider. You'll also see the search volume, by month, for searches that exactly match your entries. However, be aware that the numbers are rounded. What does that mean?

- The results are rounded to the nearest 10. The number 10 is the smallest possible result and likely means the search volume is 5 to 14.
- A blank or dash does not necessarily indicate that no searches have been performed for your keywords, but it does mean that the number is fewer than 10.

Other Tips:

- The higher the search volume, the more competition you'll have for the keyword or phrase.
- Generally, the more words you add to your phrase, the lower the search volume.
- For content optimization, you want to find specific terms that have 10 or more searches. Searches in the 100s may be viable contenders. Searches in the 1,000s probably will not be.
- The competitive rankings of "low," "medium" and "high" refer to advertising purchases, not organic search.

Question #2: Do I have a chance to rank for the keywords?

I wish I could tell you that the second question is as easy to answer as the first. No such luck. Intuition is involved, and experience will help.

There is, however, another tool — two, actually — that you can rely on to help answer this question. Both come from the company Moz and are available in a free version with ample functionality. The first of these, Open Site Explorer, can be accessed via the web. The tool will report the current domain authority, or DA, which is an important factor in this exercise. Simply enter your domain (or a competitor's) to find your DA as well as a backlink profile. You'll also receive a page authority (PA) for the specific page you've queried.

Your second critical tool is MozBar, a free Chrome extension. Install MozBar and toggle it on when needed. Next, perform a Google search. You'll see the SERP, as usual, but also page and domain authority for each result. Data regarding links to the page will also be presented.

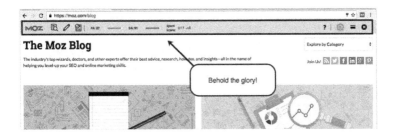

OK, that's how you GET the numbers. Here's how you APPLY them... When you examine the results of your keyword searches, what you're hoping to find are some DA scores near yours, preferably below. So, if your DA is 40, and Page 1 is entirely dominated by competitors with DAs of 50 and above, you may not have a lost cause, but you have a much steeper slope to climb.

SEO mastermind Andy Crestodina likens this to "entering the wrong race." He says you can't win at Indy on a bicycle, but you'll win a foot race every time on a bike. So, ideally, you want to avoid insurmountable competition. Among the ranking pages for your target phrase, try to find SERP results containing one or more LOWER domain authority rankings. There could be a place for your page here.

Long-Tail Keywords

Keywords come in two types: broad and long-tail. Long-tail keywords are the key to success and here's why. Broad (sometimes called "head" or "seed") keywords are short words or phrases, usually one or two words. Competition for these keywords is likely to be remarkably high, which makes your chance of ranking for them much lower.

Long-tail keywords are longer phrases that are more specific. While search volume for long-tail keywords will be lower, your ability to earn high rankings for them will go up. Your conversion rate is likely to rise, too, because a long-tail search generally brings in more relevant and qualified traffic. Think about how a search for the word "guitar" would compare with "used Taylor acoustic steel string guitar." It's easy to see how the latter keyword phrase suggests the searcher has a better idea of the product he seeks.

Targeting long-tail keywords is akin to the "big fish in a small pond" strategy. It makes far more sense for most content optimizers, especially for those that do not have highly trafficked sites with high authority and rankings.

Question #3: Can I make the best page on the web for this topic?

Take a close look at the search result pages for any keywords or keyword phrases you're targeting. How does the content stack up with yours? What can you do differently that will attract readers in droves?

Chances are, the pages that rank on Page 1 are there for a reason and may have been there for some time. Your goal is to budge one of them onto Page 2, making room for your content. It won't be easy. What must you do? You need to create the best content, with the best approach, story, insights and other elements of success that multiply your chances in a very big way.

Here are some variables or factors you tend to find on the highest-ranking pages:

- **Depth** — Shallow stories are sliding off Page 1 fast and giving way to well-researched, well-written content assets that are deep. In most cases, they are lengthier than in years past. High-ranking blog posts are usually 2,000 words or more. But they're not long and fluffy. They're informative.

- **Semantic phrases** — Whether purposeful or accidental, high-ranking pages and posts include not only specific keywords, but also a number of semantically related phrases. You probably don't need to overthink this. Just write naturally. However, you might use keyword research tools to discover the phrases that are often associated with your keywords.

- **Links** — Your links should point to related content on your website and other high-authority sources and websites. Look at Wikipedia for examples of how it's done.

- **Authority** — You can improve your own authority by linking to other authoritative websites and webpages. But too much linking or linking to non-contextually related sites can hurt your authority. The best way to build authority is to create content assets that people WANT to link to.

Advanced SEO

Here are a few advanced SEO techniques from highly accomplished digital marketer and entrepreneur Neil Patel:

- Audit your site framework. Use Quicksprout.com to analyze your site's performance and fix its errors.
- Spy on and target competitors' live keywords. Use SEMRush and BacklinkWatch.com to identify the keywords your competitors rank for.
- Do research via Quora. Extract new content ideas by analyzing the results from searches for relevant keywords on

this question-and-answer site.
- Create infographics and submit them to top infographic directories such as Slideshare, Visual.ly and Infographics Archive.

 Content Strategy MasterClass Resource Appendix:
Reference to Neil Patel's complete list of 10 advanced SEO techniques.

Avoid Black Hat Tactics

A lot of so-called SEO wisdom is dated and dangerous. It's important to understand which tactics are acceptable ("white hat," as they're called), and which are not (known as "black hat"). Here are some "black hat" strategies to avoid:

Keyword stuffing: Writers (even SEO professionals) might overdo the use of keywords in a misguided effort to appeal to search engines, not realizing that search engines can detect when keywords are overused. So write content naturally. The best reader experience turns out to be the best strategy for search engine optimization as well.

Invisible links: Another bogus tactic is to embed text/links that are invisible to readers but picked up by search engines.

"Cloaking": Cloaking is an attempt to trick search engines by serving them an SEO-enhanced version of a webpage that is different from the version served to readers. As you might suspect, cloakers are often found out and penalized.

Link exchanges: Many companies neglect ethical linking standards, instead offering seedy link exchanges. Avoid them. Do due diligence. Again, do not fall for any strategy that builds links strictly for SEO purposes.

SEO Conclusion

Remember, one of your most important goals as a content strategist is to get your client's content discovered via search. Organic search may be the most important channel in digital marketing. Optimizing for search engines, especially Google, is an essential best practice. Nearly two-thirds of all the online search queries in the world are done through Google — an average of 1 billion searches every month. Apply the basics of SEO found in this section, along with topic and content optimization, and you'll be well on your way.

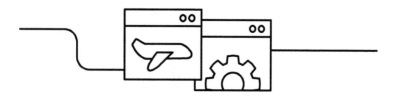

II. LANDING PAGE OPTIMIZATION

Your important keywords are now intelligently featured and your content is fully optimized for search engines, but your job is not over yet. All your great content will be published on a webpage that you also will need to optimize for readers as well as search engines. This could be a page already on your site or a new landing page developed specifically for a campaign.

You'll need to understand the proper places to put keywords on the page for two reasons: 1) so that the search engine will understand the page's content; and 2) so that readers will find the content with ease. When you understand how to use keywords as on-page signals for content optimization, you'll find that your CMS, or content management system (as well as a variety of convenient plugin options), will make it easy to optimize your pages without your having to touch the underlying HTML ("hypertext markup language") code. On most CMS platforms, such as WordPress, a series of prompts will remind you to optimize your pages effectively.

Let's run through the instances in which you'll apply the use of keywords:

Title Tags

<title>

Creating a title for each page you publish tells search engines what the page is about. The use of the word "tag" or "tags" refers to how the title will appear in the HTML code, sandwiched between a "less than" (<) symbol and a "greater than" (>) symbol: <title>. Naturally, you'll want to use keywords in your title tag for best optimization practice. In fact, your page title is the most prominent and most important place to apply keywords, which can be one or more words. Keywords must be chosen carefully and used as naturally as possible.

Take a look at any SERP and you'll see titles of pages listed. Because the character count of a title is limited, some titles will be truncated so that they end with an ellipsis, or dot-dot-dot, indicating the title tag is longer than the space allows. It's wise to avoid this problem when possible by limiting titles to 60 characters or, better yet, 55. It's also wise to ensure your keywords appear at the beginning or near the beginning of the title; that will ensure that they are seen not only by the search engine but also by the user. Most CMS systems offer a preview feature that helps you visualize how your title will be rendered on a SERP.

H Tags

    <h1>
    <h2>
    <h3>

"H" is for headline. H tags represent a hierarchy of headlines that reflect formatting choices you've made for the page's main headline (H1) and subordinate headlines or subheads (H2, H3 and so on).

Your H1, or headline, often is the same as your title. However, you can choose to make it different, maybe a variation of your title that you'd like readers to see, even though it runs longer than the allotted character count for titles. For instance, you could follow a short headline with a parenthetical statement that appears on the page as part of the headline, but that is not treated as the title by the search engine.

A few tips to consider…

- **Use only one H1 line per page.** Multiple H1s will confuse the search engine.
- **You can use multiple H2s, and you should.** It's important to break up your page content with subheads, and keywords in your subheads are likely to also serve as relevance indicators.

You can continue with H tags and apply H3 and H4 phrases. These may call attention to keywords in lists or bolded subsections.

Image Tags

<img>

Though search engines read words, not pictures or videos, search engines do "serve" images and videos on SERPs. In fact, they dedicate a separate, and usually large, list of pages to images that are discovered via search. Images are tagged with keywords, much as headlines are. When you upload images for placement on your pages, the CMS prompts you to tag them appropriately.

The first of the two tags, the main image tag, or "i-m-g," will probably be automatically populated with the filename and format. You can leave this alone.

More important is what's called the "alt" tag. You'll want to describe the image and use your keywords in the description. For example, a post about how to barbecue a juicy hamburger may include a photo of the hamburger tagged with "how to barbecue a juicy hamburger."

Using keywords in the "alt" tag probably is not going to make or break your content optimization effort, but it's indeed another opportunity to indicate relevance and follow any and all of the SEO best practices.

Meta Descriptions

<meta description>

Meta descriptions are the all-important content optimization element that is all too often misunderstood and neglected. When you perform a search, the results you're served include a description of the page (or at least they should). This is the meta description, commonly called a "snippet." Search engines look for these snippets, as they do all relevance indicators, in the code. Your challenge is to create a meta description for a web page that summarizes the content on the page. Think of what you write as a little ad about your page. When presented to a reader, the description should persuade the reader to click through.

Meta descriptions have limited space. Your CMS will encourage you to limit the description to 160 characters and warn you if you exceed it.

The meta description structure isn't perfect. Meta descriptions do not always appear in the search results. Sometimes, the search engine pulls content directly from the page, bolding the words on the page that match the searcher's keyword phrase.

URLs

www.keywords-in-the-URL.com/likehere/andhere

Even the URL of the page itself is subject to content optimization. The best practice for web page optimization is to include keywords in the URL if possible.

A lot of variations come into play here, and some are more technical than others. Sites such as WordPress simply include the title of your blog post in the URL string. Large e-commerce sites often include the product name in the URL by default.

Typically, you'll find that each word is separated by a hyphen to improve readability. When possible, be selective and use only the most important keywords or phrases that best explain what's on the page, avoiding any unimportant words or phrases.

Headlines

Optimizing your headlines helps snag readers and casual browsers, enticing them to learn the answers, find out what or why, and read on to learn more. The best content strategists dedicate immense time and effort to create headlines with pulling power that attract readers to click and continue reading.

Use tools like BuzzSumo to find out what's popular and the headlines that were used. You'll also want to experiment (A/B and multivariant testing) and reverse-engineer success by learning from readers what works, and what does not. Avoid getting too fancy or clever with your headlines. Instead, focus on clear communication of what your content will deliver, and why it's important.

Formats

Many years ago, I worked with Michael Benes, an award-winning creative director at Polaroid and later founder of Benes Communications. Michael taught me much about marketing and advertising that he had learned over the years. He understood how and why readers choose what to read, and how they read. He explained that it takes only milliseconds for readers to decide, based on the image or layout on a page, to stop their search for potential information that may or may not interest them. They then quickly browse the headline and make a decision to read on, or move on, in a second or two. Content strategists, creators and designers need to understand these core realities.

Here are a few suggestions for content formats that will draw readers to slow down and dive in.

- Let the story unfold; don't tell all the facts and conclusions up front.
- Create content with short paragraphs that are "easy on the eye."
- Add subheads to break written content into sections.
- Use numbered and bulleted lists to quickly grab attention and prioritize information.
- Use bold type and italics for emphasis, but use them sparingly.
- Use reasonably narrow column widths and ample white space.
- Use original featured images, and avoid stock photography when possible.
- Use charts, illustrations and screenshots to combat reading fatigue and sustain readers' interest.
- Write captions for images where appropriate. Skimmers love captions.
- Include video in your content if possible, one of the best ways to engage visitors and promote sharing.
- Upgrade a post with audio or produce stand-alone podcasts, a content format that is exploding in popularity.

Quotes and Mentions

Just as a reporter will include quotations to boost the credibility of a story and capture the vivid spoken language of the source, using quotations on social media can optimize your content. Andy Crestodina, co-founder of Orbit Media and author of "Content Chemistry," writes:

"If optimizing blog posts for search means adding keywords, optimizing for social means adding people. Mention experts and quote them to add credibility."

Choose influencers in your industry and repurpose quotations from their blogs, books, webinars and presentations. Quotations in general tend to be widely shared on social media. Including quotations from influencers who are relevant, inspirational, humorous or thought-provoking will help capture the interest of your readers and motivate them to share. In so doing, they will amplify your reach.

 Content Strategy MasterClass Resource Appendix:
Reference to Andy Crestodina's book "Content Chemistry."

Best Content for Landing Page Optimization

Here are a few proven ideas for engaging and connecting with readers that you can use to improve your landing pages:

- Buyers or Info Seekers. In his keynote at Content Marketing World, Andy Crestodina suggested that we design all our content and web pages with two distinct groups in mind: Buyers and Info Seekers. The two groups have different needs that drive the type and style of content you create, optimize and publish.
- Opinionated Content. As it turns out, readers are interested in authors' opinions that help define who they are and what they stand for. Content is more likely to be remembered and passed around if you can make a "connection" through your opinions on a topic.
- Researched Content. Another type of content that performs well with readers and search engines is content that is well researched, referencing reputable sources and authorities on the topic. Creating this type of content starts with a question that the content answers.
- Insights. Let's face it: We all want insights that will make our life better and more fun. Insights help us upgrade our worldview, reflect on reality and deliver that flash of gold we seek when we pan for meaning. Creating content that's

insightful is challenging, however.

Here's a bit more about insights: Doug Kessler suggests we need to learn to separate facts from observations and then use both to create insights. Here's an example he showcased at Content Marketing World:

> **Fact:** People feed their pets twice a day.
> **Observation:** Pets are fed once in the AM and once in the PM.
> **Insight:** People feel guilty eating in front of their pets.

- Guest blogging. A savvy way to earn links to your landing pages is to get published as a guest blogger on other sites, preferably well-trafficked sites. While publishers are entitled to establish their own sets of rules and guidelines, most will reward your guest blog contribution by allowing you to create links to your content in your article and author bio.

- Social amplification. Landing pages that feature "popular" content that gets links and love in the social sphere are more likely to be read and shared. To boost your shares, likes and comments, you'll want to amplify your best content through paid social advertising.

Advanced Landing Page Optimization

Here are just a few tactics and techniques to improve readership and conversion rates:

Page Performance

The performance of your website refers to the technical aspects of the page, most especially the page load time. Slow-loading websites deflect readers and have a negative impact on your ranking.

SERP Stick

I learned something interesting while attending a Google presentation here in Boston a few years ago. Google rewards links on a SERP that get better click-through rates. Google penalizes a site when readers abandon its page to return to Google to seek another page that may have the answers. Great content that keeps readers on the page is essential for landing page optimization.

Freshness

It's now understood that newer content is often favored over older content. Content creators who have popular evergreen content that was published years back are wise to update it on occasion.

Search Volume

While search volume for your company, CEO or domain name may be difficult to control, SEO professionals seem to agree that it's a factor in search algorithms that determine SERP positions. Public relations strategy and tactics can help keep a brand visible with the media and on the web.

Mobile Optimization

Google began penalizing sites that were not mobile-friendly in 2015. The consensus is that mobile-optimized pages perform better for searches conducted via mobile devices, especially now that more than 50 percent of search queries globally come from mobile devices.

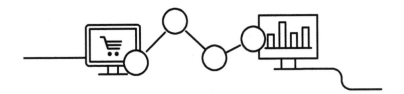

III. CONVERSION RATE OPTIMIZATION

Conversion is the ultimate measure of marketing success. Optimizing conversion is a science commonly called "conversion rate optimization" (or CRO). To increase the percentage of visitors to your website who convert into customers or who take a desired action, you must focus on this form of optimization. Conversion should be addressed all across your website — on your homepage, product pages, blog and, of course, landing pages. Let's look at some proven ways to raise conversion rates and make your content more effective.

Website Navigation

The most important consideration in increasing conversion rate optimization on your landing pages involves improving website navigation. You want visitors to your website to find what they are seeking in as few clicks or actions as possible. If visitors cannot easily navigate to find both informational content and purchase-driven assets, CRO will be impeded. To help visitors find assets easier:

- Be consistent in how and where navigation structures appear across your site.
- Make all navigation elements clickable links.
- Use accurate navigation titles. Visitors should have a general idea of what they'll find on a page even before clicking. Use accurate text to describe the linked page.
- Include only the most important or most heavily trafficked pages in your navigation bar links. For less mission-critical

links, opt for dropdown menus or other navigation structures.
- Install a website search feature.
- Invest in mobile-friendly, mobile-responsive design.
- Examine visitor flow patterns. Use this information to make tweaks to your navigation structure to subtly influence visitor behavior and boost conversions.

Benefits, Not Products and Services

The most important thing you can do to increase the conversion rate on your landing page is to know who you're targeting and to communicate the benefits in simple terms the reader will easily understand. Marketers focus too much on themselves, their brand, their products, their point of view. To affect conversion, you need to turn it around to the customer's point of view, develop a value proposition and deliver it as an answer to the question, "What's in it for me?" Get your "What's in it for me?" or WIIFM, message across by telling readers what you can do for them, not what you do.

 Benefits Exercise: An effective way to focus on benefits is to write a "how to" statement. Simply write "How to (blank)" and fill in the blank. This will prevent you from focusing on features and solutions and create a benefits-driven, customer-centric value proposition.

Social Proof

When buyers come to a crossroad in their decision-making, they look to those who have gone before them for validation. They look for what marketers call "social proof." Robert Cialdini, social psychologist and author of "Influence," writes about the powerful effect of social proof. Your aim in using social proof is to increase your prospects' trust by delivering convincing evidence that your solution has proved its merits. Some forms of social proof you'll want to use in your content to increase conversion include:

- Customer testimonials
- Numbers — such as years in business, clients served, subscriber count
- Case studies
- Press mentions
- Ratings and reviews
- Awards
- Certifications
- Social media share counts and followers
- Test results

Call to Action

The Call to Action, or CTA, is among the most important factors in conversion. You need to make CTAs work for you.

- Present your CTA as a button. This is a familiar convention. Readers are accustomed to them and know what to do.
- The words in your CTA are all-important. Begin with a verb. Make it clear what the reward of clicking will be.
- Place your CTA in a logical place in the reader's eye path.
- Use a contrasting color to make it stand out on the page.
- Giving the CTA ample breathing room also will make it stand out. Surround it with negative space to attract the readers' eyes.

Lead Magnets

An important form of conversion, especially in the B2B space, is capturing the email addresses of prospects. The best way to achieve this is to use lead magnets to make compelling offers on your website. A lead magnet is a free offer you make in exchange for an email address (and possibly information). You'll aim to convert prospects to customers by following up with lead-nurturing tactics, most notably email.

Lead magnets come in a multitude of forms. Some popular favorites are:

- E-books, guides and reports
- Checklist and cheat sheets
- Tools
- Swipe files and templates
- Quizzes and assessments
- Webinars and videos
- Discounts
- Free trials
- Product demonstrations
- Email and/or video courses

 Content Strategy MasterClass Resource Appendix: Link to the article "9 Tips for Effective Lead Magnets" by VWO.

CRO Testing Techniques: Variation and Control

A proven way to increase conversion rates is to conduct landing page tests. Such testing methods include A/B split testing and multivariate testing. A/B testing is used to determine the better of two content variations. You serve half your visitors a baseline control sample, and the other half an alternate variation. When the multivariate testing method is used, more than one content variation on a website is tested in a live environment. You might think of multivariate testing as the conducting of multiple A/B tests on one page at the same time.

Some elements worthy of testing include:

- Headlines and copy
- Layout
- Colors
- Calls-to-action
- Images
- Forms
- Offers and lead magnets
- Copy length

Conversion Rate Optimization Tools

Tools that make it easy to optimize your content for conversion come in various forms. Many are built into email and marketing automation services, while others are content-agnostic, allowing you to create tests and evaluate the results on multiple channels.

- Visual Website Optimizer is a tool we're fond of. It's easy to use and enables us to create different versions of landing pages using a point-and-click editor. The service offers additional tools such as behavioral targeting, heatmaps and usability testing.
- Optimizely is another popular option. Not only is it a robust testing tool, but the company also offers helpful resources for learning how to master A/B testing, including a book dedicated to the topic.

You can test-drive both of these paid services for free. In addition, Google offers a free service called Content Experiments for basic split testing. It comes with a setup wizard that walks you through the setting-up of experiments and helps you quickly launch new tests.

Optimization Team

Will a big budget help you optimize your content? It might. However, you now have the essential knowledge and tools needed to optimize your content yourself. Here's a quick list of experts you can hire on a freelance or full-time basis to help with optimization strategy and tactics:

- Website Auditors. Specialists and tools are available to audit your website and identify problems and opportunities.
- Keyword Researchers. Accelerate your success by partnering with keyword research experts who know how to put advanced software tools to work quickly and to identify the right keywords to focus on for search engine optimization.
- PPC Specialists. Drive more traffic to your landing pages through the advice of PPC specialists. They'll also help you amplify your content with paid advertising in the channels that matter.
- UX and UI Professionals. Websites can be complex. Professionals can optimize the user experience through the addition of navigation, images and content that transform the complex into simple solutions that win.

 Content Strategy MasterClass Resource Appendix: Tune into dozens of webinars and podcasts I've recorded over the years that will help you take your SEO to the next level.

CERTIFICATION REQUIREMENT:

In a Nutshell

Research keywords using your favorite research tool, and load them up in WriterAccess for quick access placing orders, and content analytics tracking and report on how well your keywords are performing in the search engines, and how well your content is optimized with the keywords your targeting.

Exercise

Follow these steps for keyword optimization using WriterAccess tools
1. Download Sample Keyword Map and Keyword Spreadsheet
2. Research keywords using your favorite tool like SpyFu, Moz, etc.
3. Load your keywords (and domains) into WriterAccess
  *   Click on My Tools and Tools Setup
  *   Click on Domains and Keywords
  *   Add Your Domains and Keywords
4. Place an Oder with Instruction Setup: SEO Keywords Required
  *   Click Place Order
  *   Select Instruction Setup: SEO Keywords Required
  *   View your keywords sorted by domain
  *   Add keywords to your orders

Certification Test

Then take the online Content Optimization Test

Keyword Research

Keyword research is essential if you are to aim your content in the right direction so that it will appeal to both readers and search engines. By discovering what readers are searching for and how you are performing on those searches, you can map out the topics and keywords to target that will improve your traffic, engagement and conversions.

Optimizing your content for search engines continues to be necessary for success. After all, if you're not using relevant keywords and phrases in your copy on the web, how can you make the case to search engines to get top listing for those keywords and phrases? Your keyword research will direct you to topics that are good "investments" and will improve your listing positions in the search engines.

Here are some of the elements of a keyword map that will help you zero in on the most promising keywords and topics:

Keyword Universe

This is a comprehensive list of all the keywords that drive organic traffic from the search engines to you and your competitors. And it's not just the keywords you're researching; it's the data about the keywords, including the PPC Cost, Search Volume, Ranking Difficulty and more. Building out your Keyword Universe with all the data about each keyword is the starting point for building a Keyword Map that defines your SEO strategy.

Golden Keywords

From the keyword universe can be gleaned golden keywords that are a select solar system of important keywords worthy of targeting for search engine optimization. A typical content plan limits this list to 100 keywords. The keywords may be very competitive, meaning many companies use them to drive traffic, but also be important for long-term SEO strategy.

Keyword Silos

A silo groups keywords worthy of SEO targeting by topic or some other criteria. Topic groupings help guide writers to the best topics for SEO. All your keywords work together to tell the full story of your company, brand and website. What is your brand all about? How is it relevant? How does it stand out? Why should you get top listing for keywords that matter?

 Pro Tip: Many SEO practitioners select a single keyword phrase per page and use multiple keywords from their keyword silo to support that phrase. Internal link building and cross-pollination to other pages also help with optimization. Single-page optimization strategy helps Google understand exactly what each page is about and how it relates to the whole.

Keyword Research Tools

In undertaking your keyword research, you'll find a wide array of tools, many of which also offer keyword performance reports and measurement tools.

SpyFu is an outstanding tool for keyword research. In minutes, you can learn which keywords are driving traffic to your site and to all your competition, both paid and organically, and export the data to build a keyword universe spreadsheet packed with lots of information. In hours, you can look over all the data and use the sorting tools to help select the best keywords to target for optimization and content strategy. SpyFu technology gives you all the information you need to pinpoint the winners.

SpyFu also lets you see how a company's site stacks up to the competition when it comes to organic market share, namely the listing position of your site versus the competition. All the keywords you harvest from SpyFu will list this information, giving you a good idea of how hard it will be to capture organic market share from the competition. The more your website outranks the competitors, the greater your visibility and traffic flow, increasing revenue opportunities.

Keyword Wisdom

Google's algorithm is extremely sophisticated. Not only is it unnatural to "stuff" keywords into your content, but it can actually negatively impact optimization strategy and content performance in the search engines. Instead, use keywords and keyword phrases as content themes. Include a keyword phrase once to clarify the focus of a page, but avoid excessive use of keywords throughout the copy. Go deep on the topic, reference other sources, and build authority around the theme of the keyword or keyword phrase you are using.

Expressing knowledge and insights through the use of a keyword or keyword phrase will result in content that will be shared, linked to and passed around the social sphere. This is what carries weight with the search engines.

Our content analytics tools at WriterAccess help writers use the keywords required for optimization. The tools also track the use or overuse of keywords in content.

Chapter 4:
Content Distribution

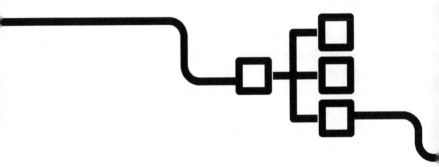

Content Distribution

Content Distribution Overview

The next step is to define the best channels for not only distributing but also amplifying your content. In this chapter, learn about alternative strategies for distributing and amplifying your content in the big three media channels: **Owned, Paid, Earned.**

These are some of the questions you will answer:

How can I get a 5X multiplier on my blog posts?
What are the secret new channels for publishing?
What's the "price" and "complexity" of core channels?
How do I find channels with my customers and prospects?
Are there any exciting new channels on the horizon?
How can I integrate product or service offers?
What's the best platform for publishing and hosting?
What's the checklist for selecting a publishing platform?

Let's start with quick definitions:

I. **Owned media** is the channel you own and manage with full control — your website, blog, social media accounts, marketing content and other assets.
II. **Paid media** is the channel, operating with specific rules and guidelines beyond your control, that you pay to push out your content or promotions to reach a targeted audience — advertorials, sponsorships, pay-per-click, display and paid social.
III. **Earned media** is the channel you earn through the quality of your content, story, solutions or opinion that get shared, for the most part, beyond your control — likes, shares,

press mentions, positive reviews, comments, reposts, recommendations, features and other positive word of mouth.

The three media channels overlap and intertwine, so the key to optimizing your content asset distribution lies in understanding how paid and social channels can reinforce each other's benefits. Each channel has particular strengths, weaknesses and challenges in meeting the needs of the target audience. But when you cross-pollinate successfully, you can get a lot more bang for your buck, drive more shares and traffic, reach your audience, and succeed with earned media — the best and most valuable distribution channel.

You, the content strategist, must develop plans that enable you to invest your budget, time and energy wisely to get the best results from each content asset in each channel.

I. OWNED MEDIA

Owned media includes content you publish and distribute on media channels you own, such as your website, blog and social media accounts. Here are a few of the many benefits of owned media:

- Publishing Control. For the majority of owned media, you benefit from complete control of the content, including quality, quantity, frequency and link strategy.

- Cost Efficiency. You're living in the Dark Ages if you're not tapping into the next generation of publishing platforms that are, for the most part, free. The technology just keeps getting better and better, giving you more power to publish and share.
- Brand Identity. You are what you publish, giving you the opportunity to let your readers and fans learn about who you are, what you represent and how you can help people make their lives better.
- Timeless Content. The content you publish on your own website and even in the social sphere is timeless. Paid media, in contrast, abruptly ends the instant your budget runs out.
- Strategic Versatility. Because you're in control of what you publish, how it's linked, and even how it's published, with A/B testing and more, you're in the driver's seat when it comes to content strategy for all your owned media.

Website and Blog

Let's start by considering advice and a few tips for two of the most popular owned media, your website and blog:

- Content Quality. The better your content, the more "viral" and successful you will be in expanding your reach beyond your own channel. And that's true for all your channels.

- Publishing Frequency. The publishing world is built around consistency: Publishing daily, weekly and/or monthly demonstrates your ability to feed your readers and fans the information they want and need with consistency. The search engines also recognize and reward publishing frequency; the bots "learn" your publishing habits as they crawl the web to index everything new so it's searchable for all.

- Cross-Pollination. Linking within your owned channel is another tactic designed for both readers and search engines.

Linking to similar content on other pages of your website helps readers dive deeper into the topic or related topics. Links within your owned media also help the search engines better understand the content on the page. But remember not to pollute your pollination with too many links.

- Optimizing Links. Because you own and manage the content on all the media you own, you can optimize links for both readers and search engines. Doing so will give you the biggest bang for your buck.

- Multi-Channel Creation. When you're creating a blog post or article that's worthy of sharing and promoting in other media channels, be sure to create the social versions at the time you're creating the content, building "distribution" strategy into the creation process. At WriterAccess, our customers can "add on" Tweets or Facebook posts to blog posts; for just a few dollars more, the social versions will be delivered with the original blog post order.

It's up to you, the content strategist, to make sure all of the above happens to maximize your company's content distribution reach.

Blogging

Your blog is the central hub of your owned media strategy. Make sure your blog encourages sharing and engagement.

- Integrate your blog with a "social style" comments section such as Disqus, Livefyre or even Facebook comments.
- Add social sharing buttons. (The type that remain onscreen as the reader scrolls perform best.)
- Use eye-catching images that are worthy of sharing on Pinterest (or anywhere).
- Create pre-populated tweets with clicktotweet.

Social

The best channels to get content out and traffic in are most likely your social media platforms. In a sense, you own and control these channels, giving you an opportunity to employ a few tactics to grow and scale their reach and performance.

Let's start by listing the social channels you need to explore, listed by popularity (number of users as of the publishing of this book). Be aware that new channels are launched on a regular basis, and that channels are retired just as often.

Platform	Active Users
Facebook	1.7B
YouTube	1B
WhatsApp	1B
Tumblr	555M
Instagram	500M
Twitter	313M
Baidu Tieba	300M
Skype	300M
Sina Weibo	282M
Viber	249M
Reddit	234M
Line	218M
Vine	200M
YY	122M
LinkedIn	106M
Pinterest	100M
Snapchat	100M
Flickr	100M
Medium	30M
Periscope	5M
Slack	3M

Tips for Social

Here are a few tips, tactics and techniques to consider as you distribute your content in the social channels:

- **When in Rome.** Do as the Romans Do. Every social media channel has its own language. The type of post, length of text or lack of text, use of images, slang, hashtags, tagging, protocol for shares and comments, and vernacular vary greatly by platform. Tread lightly, always spending some time observing the habits of other fans and followers before diving in with your own content.

- **Reverse-Engineer Success.** While some say it's difficult to predict what will get shared, liked or passed around in the social sphere, WordStream founder Larry Kim is not one of them. Kim, who tracks and monitors viral content in the social sphere, suggests that a lot can be learned from those success stories that can be applied to new campaigns.

 Content Strategy MasterClass Resource Appendix: Watch the webinar with BuzzSumo director Steve Rayson: "How to Go Viral: Lessons From the Most Shared Content of 2015."

- **The Science of Social Sharing.** The New York Times did an interesting survey on why people share. The survey concluded that we tend to share content that we think our friends and fans will like and share. This makes content creation challenging, as we don't really know the fan base of the friends we connect with in the social sphere.

- **A Picture Says a Thousand Words.** And sometimes, it might entice a thousand shares.

- **Sight, Sound and Motion.** YouTube's stranglehold on video is over. Video dominates the social sphere and is becoming the favored medium of Facebook. It's growing in popularity on many other channels as well. And in many instances, it's the reason for the channel's existence. Experiment with social video and don't fuss unnecessarily with production values, except to be sure to capture quality audio.

- **Ego Bait.** Social platforms are designed to be social, in a variety of ways. Mentions, retweets, shares and more contribute to the social merry-go-round. Take the opportunity to connect with influencers by using social tags such as @ , +, like, share, retweet and hashtags.

- **Link Love.** As mentioned, linking strategy is now an important tactic for social content strategy. Most, but not all, of the social platforms allow you to add links. Instagram does not. Wherever possible, include links to the content you're promoting. Your link is your call to action as well as your optimization trigger.

- **Timing Is Everything.** Look into the published data regarding the best time to post to maximize sharing and boost your social clout. Who knows? Perhaps you can trigger the next viral campaign. Timing may not be critical, but it's worth considering.

- **Automate, Automate, Automate.** There are so many tools to help automate your social publishing: Buffer, ITTT, Sprout Social, Postplanner, Meet Edgar…The list is long. Many CMS plugins also will facilitate and schedule sharing. And sharing functionality is built into platforms such as HubSpot, ScoopIt and others. If possible,   automate some of your publishing efforts to increase your efficiency. But stay natural and real for true social distribution.

- **More Tricks of the Trade.** Every social network has its own bag of tricks. For instance, Twitter cards require a little extra effort to set up, but pay off when it comes to performance. Scour the Help sections for best practices, and find expert bloggers who offer need-to-know productivity hacks.

Podcasts

Commuters, exercisers, busy moms and dads all want content, but don't always have time to read books and blogs or watch video. For them, podcasting, the ultimate multitasker-friendly medium, has become a popular alternative. And it's equally friendly for producers, because podcasts are easy to record and allow you to really connect with your audience.

Before recording your first podcast, make a small investment in a good microphone. Register for a podcast hosting service and syndicate your podcast to iTunes, Stitcher and other popular outlets. Also, be sure to publish your podcasts on your blog along with episode notes, and encourage listeners to comment on and share the installments they like.

Email Marketing

Email remains the most popular medium in business today, making it the top content distribution tactic for most marketers. To succeed, you need to build a significant email database, master the tools to manage email in volume, and persuade recipients to open, read and click-through. As you develop your email chops, consider some of the many forms of potentially effective email opportunities beyond the newsletter, including triggered emails, autoresponder series and transactional email.

Can email be considered a paid medium? Perhaps. Though marketers generally do pay for email services, the services are inexpensive and the value's really in the list. So we're going to call email an owned medium.

Employee Advocacy

Employees may be the most overlooked content promotion strategy. Your employees are your ultimate content promoters, especially if they work directly with customers. Getting them to help with social distribution can be challenging, but it is worth the effort to train and educate them in how and when to share, and why it's important for the brand. Getting your entire team involved in content creation, event planning and/or performance tracking will give them a feeling of ownership, which in turn leads to even more sharing. Ask employees to contribute ideas and have them help create the content or create it for them.

Repurposing Content

Creating content is hard work. And, as you've learned in this workbook, distributing it takes even more time and money. That's why savvy content marketers are avid practitioners of content repurposing. By repurposing your content for multiple channels, platforms and audiences, you will give it new life and expose it to more readers and fans.

Examples of smart repurposing plays are nearly endless. For instance, a detailed how-to post written originally for your blog can be repurposed as an infographic, podcast, video, e-book, cheat sheet, SlideShare, webinar and other uses.

The Sum Is Always Greater Than the Parts. One of my favorite tactics is to create and publish content that facilitates a "roll up" of the content into an e-book or printed book. Check out the services that help you quickly create e-books from blog posts — a very handy tactic for creating lead magnets to build your email list.

 Content Strategy MasterClass Resource Appendix:
Link to a guide by Co-Schedule called "50+ Places to Repurpose Your Content: The Ultimate Guide."

II. PAID MEDIA

My introduction to content marketing was a book published by best-selling author and marketer Seth Godin in which he declared, "The only marketing left is content marketing." Content marketing authorities sometimes proclaim that advertising has died, with claims like "big brains beat big budgets." And while they likely can offer examples to support the claim, the reality is that paid media has not died; it's evolved.

Let's explore some paid media options, platforms and tactics as we dive deeper.

Paid Media Benefits

Paid media — advertising, sponsorships and paid promotions — deliver quite a few compelling benefits:

1. Immediacy — You can gain instant traction with paid media programs.
2. Control — You call the shots and control your exposure and budget.
3. Targeted — You can laser-focus your reach.
4. Scalable — You can scale up programs that are delivering results and dial down the ones that are coming up short.

When making any ad buy, you need to answer a few key questions to help you dive in quickly and start experimenting at a fairly low cost:

- **Target Audience.** How granular can you get?
- **Ad Spend.** What is your monthly budget?
- **Tricks of the Trade.** Are there any? What do the pros do?
- **Getting Started.** What is the URL to place my first ad?
- **Service and Support.** Are there any?

Paid Media Tactics

Here are a few tips, tactics and techniques to consider for paid media:

- **Acorns and Oak Trees.** It's all about getting the biggest bang for your buck when it comes to content marketing. The key to that is testing and learning which content will draw a crowd and be shared. To achieve that goal, you'll want to use your owned media to learn what works and then amplify that content via paid media in the social sphere. It's a bit like planting lots of acorns, knowing that only a few will grow into oak trees with the right soil, water conditions and environment.

- **Remove the Emotion.** I've spent a lot of money unwisely promoting content that I personally loved but that did not perform, get shared or transform browsers into buyers. Let performance be the driver for spending decisions. Start small and learn what works and does not work.

- **Creation/Amplification Ratio.** To produce high-quality content worthy of amplification, you need to raise the bar and spend more on creation. Once you develop great content, ramp up the paid spend budget to maximize the initial creative investment. Maintaining this creation-amplification balance is the responsibility of the content strategist. The only way to learn this art/science is to be granted the budget to experiment and learn about the audience.

Paid Media and Facebook

Since its launch in 2005, when early adopters were able to generate huge fan bases simply by setting up a page, Facebook has evolved into a paid media channel. "Pay to play" is a phrase that surfaces in most conversations about Facebook pages today, because, for brands, organic reach on Facebook has dwindled.

The Facebook advertising program is robust and far-reaching. Provided your page has earned 50 likes, you can get started for as little as $5. Facebook offers various types of ads that let you promote your page, website or individual posts. Facebook's "boosted posts" present many options for reaching people who like your page, their friends and new audiences. You can promote posts from your news feed, timeline or page, including status updates, photos, videos and offers.

 Content Strategy MasterClass Resource Appendix: Link to the Facebook Advertising Help Center can assist you in getting started with paid programs.

Paid Media and Twitter

Twitter has become the go-to social platform for more than 300 million fans who look to it for news, stories, announcements and updates, both local and worldwide. Brands also are tapping into this revolutionary channel. There are three ways to promote your tweets and nine ad types on Twitter (as of October 2016).

Tweet Promotion

Promoted Tweets: Similar to a boosted post on Facebook, you add a few dollars behind a favorite piece of content to get more eyes on your tweet.

Promoted Accounts: Includes a short description about why someone should follow your account and provides an easy "Follow" button within the tweet for anyone interested in doing so.

Promoted Trends: Sends your hashtag to the top of the trending hashtag list in certain locations. This is probably one of the most expensive Twitter options and will be provided only if it fits within the monthly budget you shared with the media platform.

Twitter Ad Types

1. App Card

Brands that have a mobile application use this type of ad to drive app installs. When users click on the ad, they go to the app store for download. This offering includes space for a title, description, icon and app rating or price.

2. Lead Generation Card

Businesses that want to collect highly qualified leads on Twitter use this type of ad to capture email addresses to grow their databases.

3. Photo Card

Now called the "summary card with large image," the photo card allows you to put a full-width image, title, description and link alongside your desired tweet. Clicking on the image will take the user to your website, unlike an organic tweet, which will expand the image to a full-screen version of your tweet. This ad type is ideal for increasing web traffic for campaigns that rely on visual content.

4. Gallery Card

This type of ad is similar to the photo card, but it allows your brand to showcase a variety of products or images from your website to give them a preview of what they will find when they click-through.

5. Website Card

Businesses trying to increase web traffic use this type of ad to send users to any website or landing page they desire. The card has space for a horizontal image, text, link and a call-to-action button, and has garnered impressive results.

6. Player Card

A place for music, video or GIFs you want to share as part of your marketing campaign. This is one of the most effective cards to encourage users to watch, listen and click-through to your content.

7. Summary Card

As organic tweets, these usually come up in a search only when the user has included a link in addition to the text — almost like a "default" tweet. This card includes a title, description, thumbnail image and a direct link to your content.

8. Product Card

This is the best ad option for retailers to show off their products. It has space for an image, description of up to 200 characters, product details, and price or stock availability.

9. Conversational Card

Conversational cards take promoted tweets to a whole new level by including a call-to-action button with customizable hashtags. When the button is clicked, a pre-populated message designed by your brand pops up for the user to tweet and help continue the conversation.

Because there are so many options, Twitter has grouped them into four campaigns and will walk you through your goals to help you find the right ad format for you.

1. **Website Clicks:** Increase site visits, conversions and sales.
2. **Followers:** Build an audience.
3. **Engagement:** Increase retweets, likes and mentions.
4. **App:** Increase downloads and app engagement.

You can tailor your campaigns to your business goals and target non-followers by using many variables to dictate where your sponsored tweets appear. There is no minimum spend, and you pay only when a user engages with your promoted tweet.

Paid Media and LinkedIn

LinkedIn Marketing Solutions targets professionals and includes advertising options to help build your brand, raise awareness and generate leads. Reach just the right audience with comprehensive targeting options. Set your own budget and choose from cost-per-click or cost-per-impression options.

Self Service

LinkedIn's self-service solutions let you launch a targeted campaign in minutes. You can set your own budget, choose clicks or impressions, and stop your ads at any time using Campaign Manager, LinkedIn's all-in-one advertising platform. Campaign Manager supports sponsored content and text ads.

- **Sponsored Content —** Boost your content to a large professional audience.
- **Text Ads —** Drive high-quality leads within your budget via a self-service advertising platform.

Managed Campaigns

LinkedIn's account-managed advertising allows you to partner with a dedicated LinkedIn team to create exclusively placed, highly visible ads for premium audiences. Its team will help you fine-tune your targeting and create personalized content that converts. Account-managed ad formats include sponsored content, sponsored inmail, dynamic ads and display ads, along with account-based marketing using LinkedIn account targeting.

- **Sponsored Content —**
  Boost your content to a large professional audience.
- **Sponsored InMail —**

Reach your target audience via content in their LinkedIn inboxes.

- **Dynamic Ads** —
  Grab attention with dynamically generated, personalized display ads.
- **Display Ads** —
  Run display campaigns that drive brand awareness and keep you on prospects' minds.

 Content Strategy MasterClass Resource Appendix: Link to the LinkedIn Marketing Solutions.

Paid Media and YouTube

Any video uploaded to YouTube can be an ad. Video ads appear before other videos on YouTube, beside videos that are playing, and in search results. YouTube ads use a pay-per-view model. You pay only when your ad is watched. Video ads are powered by Google AdWords, so you'll need an account, which is free.

The 10 video ad options on YouTube are:

1. Desktop Video Mastheads
2. Mobile Video Mastheads
3. Rich Media Masthead — Custom Implementation
4. Rich Media Masthead — Layouts Implementation
5. Video Ads (formerly In-Stream Video Ads)
6. TrueView In-Stream Ads
7. TrueView Video Discovery Ads
8. Standard Display Ads
9. In-Video Overlay Ads
10. Live Streaming in Ads

With so many ad options, you can tailor your daily budget to a spend you're comfortable with. Plus, you pay only when someone engages with your ad; if a viewer skips it before 30 seconds (or the end), you don't pay a cent. YouTube has targeting options that help you reach the right customer for your business. You can target by age, gender, location, interests and other factors. YouTube has built-in analytics that make it easy to see how your ad performs. You can also make adjustments to your ad at any time and even run multiple ads at once to see which works best.

 Content Strategy MasterClass Resource Appendix: Link to the You Tube Advertiser Center and Google Display Ad Specs.

Native Advertising

Native advertising is a relatively new form of paid media in which the ad experience follows the natural form and function of the user experience. This means your ad looks and feels like the content around it. Most online publishers offer native advertising programs. Though your content will be "branded," it will largely match the non-sponsored content beside, above and below it.

In most cases, native advertising is commingled with standard content in a fairly seamless way, although some publishers create specific sections for this type of content. While native advertising is seldom a low-cost endeavor, it will afford you the opportunity to put your content before a large and highly targeted audience in a less intrusive and more compelling manner.

Here are 12 examples of native advertising from Copyblogger Media:

1. Print advertorials
2. Online advertorials
3. Online video advertorials
4. Advertorial... gone wrong
5. Sponsored content
6. Single-sponsor issues

7. Branded content

8. Product placement

9. In-feed ads

10. Sponsored posts (Facebook)

11. Promoted tweets

12. Google text ads (search listings)

 Content Strategy MasterClass Resource Appendix: Link to a post by CopyBlogger featuring examples of native ads.

Discovery Services

Paid content distribution networks offered by discovery services have broadened marketers' distribution options.

Outbrain   Outbrain

Outbrain describes its service as the leading content discovery platform on the web. The company's "Amplify" service will distribute your content on the websites of 300+ premium publishers. Outbrain currently operates strictly on a Cost-per-Click, or CPC, pricing model. This means that you set an amount that you're willing to pay for every click to your content.

For example, if you have a $25 campaign with a 45-cent CPC, this means you are willing to pay 45 cents for every click you get until you hit your $25 budget cap — so your maximum traffic potential is 56 clicks. You can always change your CPC depending on how well you're performing.

 Content Strategy MasterClass Resource Appendix: Link to the Outbrain Resource Center.

Taboola

Taboola's service is very similar to Outbrain's. Taboola claims its service makes 40 billion recommendations monthly using its "Content You May Like" tagline, and that this staggering volume has resulted in 400 million unique users monthly. Taboola offers a CPC pricing model. Since you pay only when your content is clicked on, this means your charges will vary from month to month.

 Content Strategy MasterClass Resource Appendix:
Link to the Taboola Resource Center.

Adblade

Another player in the paid article distribution space, Adblade, reaches more than 300 million unique users in the U.S. each month. Adblade offers both CPC and CPM (cost-per-thousand views) pricing.

 Content Strategy MasterClass Resource Appendix:
Link to the Adblade Resource Center.

StumbleUpon

Over 35 million people use StumbleUpon to discover content. StumbleUpon's paid discovery program puts your URL into users' streams, directing traffic directly to the page you choose.

StumbleUpon Ads is a native advertising platform that does not use traditional ad units such as banners or text links. On StumbleUpon, your ad is, quite simply, your URL. Since your webpage itself is the ad unit, no additional creative assets or copy is needed to drive traffic. Visitors go directly to your page when they click the Stumble button. Your ad appears during a user's stumble session. Each time they click the "Stumble" button on their StumbleBar, the site recommends a new webpage. Some of the pages they stumble upon will be from advertisers. Sponsored stumbles look and behave just like any other stumble but are indicated with a sponsored label in the StumbleBar.

Ad Cost: StumbleUpon charges 5 cents for each paid stumble, or view, delivered through StumbleUpon ads. It does not charge for additional views that result from sharing or from members finding your page organically.

Content Strategy MasterClass Resource Appendix:
Link to the StumbleUpon Ads Resource Center.

reddit

Describing itself as "the front page of the Internet," reddit is visually crude and hard to understand, so it's not for everybody. However, it's common for the site to receive 6 billion pageviews in a month. You can promote your content on reddit with promoted posts targeting any of reddit's many communities (called "subreddits"). Use the search tool or click on one of the "hot," "rising" or "new" tabs at the top to find relevant subreddits.

Self-Service Ad Platform: With reddit's self-serve platform, you can launch promoted posts targeting any reddit community.

What you'll need to get started:
- reddit account
- Ad copy
- Click-through URL or text to promote
- 70x70 thumbnail (optional, but recommended)

To begin, log in to your reddit account. If you don't have an account, create one by going to reddit.com and clicking the "log-in or sign-up" link in the top right corner. When creating your account, be sure to include your email address. You will need to verify this address when submitting payment for your ad. You will be notified via this email address upon submission, launch and completion of your ad.

To create a promotion, scroll to the bottom of any reddit page and click on the "advertise" link, or go directly to reddit.com/advertising in your browser. On this page, click the "create an ad" button. You will be directed to the reddit advertising platform, which will prompt you to create your ad. On the first page, you can upload your thumbnail image, create a title for your promotion, choose the type of promotion you'd like to launch ("post type"), and provide the URL for the ad.

Ad Cost: Reddit is currently offering a flat 75-cent CPM for self-serve advertising — you'll get the same price regardless of the choices you make in targeting or content. There is a minimum buy of $5 for any individual sponsored link (which you'll also have to pay for individually).

 Content Strategy MasterClass Resource Appendix:
Link to the Reddit Self Service Resource Center.

III. EARNED MEDIA ☆☆☆

Earned media is the hardest channel to tackle, but it can deliver the biggest rewards. Think of it as a form of public relations, namely, strategic communication that seeks public opinion and builds strong sentiment with a brand's customers, prospects, employees and fans. Traditional public relations focuses on targeting media outlets, industry publications, award shows and other mainstream channels. But the expanding digital world has opened up new channels of communication with the public such as social media, review forums, online publishers, thought leaders, influencers and others.

Earned media now is understood to include any content published without "pay to the author" or "barter exchange" or "fringe benefits" that might influence public opinion. This channel can certainly be murky when it comes to identifying earned media content and quantifying its benefit. Nevertheless, the value of public opinion is priceless and its impact on buying decisions cannot be discounted, especially when the influence stems from a trusted, authoritative source.

Earned Media: Benefits

Earned media has benefits galore, making the effort to achieve it worth the time and investment.

- **Cost/Reward Ratio.** By definition, earned media has no fee paid to the author of the story, article or mention of you or your brand. You earn that recognition by originating the idea, story, strategy, policy, plan or tactic that triggers the published opinion. There is arguably a cost to forge the strategy and execute the tactics to achieve earned media coverage. But the goal is to minimize those costs and maximize the reward.

- **Verified Credible.** The more credible the source, the higher the reward. Credibility typically is determined not by some magical third party, but by the readership, trust and loyalty of the publisher's fan base. The larger that base, the more credible the publisher — and the greater the reach and rewards for the brand.

- **Evergreen Value.** Unlike paid programs, which vanish after they expire, earned media often has longstanding residual value, remaining on the web long after the original mention, story or opinion has been passed around.

- **Customer Voice.** In today's "shout it out" and "share it all" world, the customer is now on center stage, armed with public opinion tools such as Glassdoor and Yelp. These tools can instantly spread feedback about your business, service, products or experience with your brand. In a recent study, 90 percent of respondents stated that online reviews influence their buying decisions. Fully 58 percent said they were more likely to share customer service experiences today than they were five years ago, with greater numbers sharing experiences on social networking sites and writing online reviews.

 Content Strategy MasterClass Resource Appendix: Link to a Marketing Land article about frustrations over untimely customer service resolution.

- **Multi-Tiered Reach.** Earned media helps you expand your reach to new prospects and customers in many ways. The original mention reaches the audience/fan base of the publisher. If the content is shared by that audience, your reach expands. Marketing the content to your audience will help influence your own base. And if your audience shares the content, you grow your reach even more.

Earned Media: Tactics

Earned media is not a get-rich-quick scheme. Your earned media strategy starts with deeper initiatives and tactics that define who you are, what you stand for and believe in, and why you're worthy of public mention and support. Here's a quick overview to get you started, sourced with the help of Barry Feldman:

Brand Stand: Brands have public personas built on the thoughts, opinions and feelings that customers have developed about them. What is your vision? What are your core values? What is your strategic plan? How do you make life better? How do you treat people? What is your secret sauce that drives growth? These answers form the public perception of the brand. While earned media can help shape that perception, core values must be where the perception starts.

Owning Earned: Who's going to "own" earned media strategy and tactics in your company? Outsourcing the task to a next-gen public relations firm or an influencer marketing agency is one possibility, but your content strategist is likely to be the hero here again: gathering ideas, motivating thought leaders, nurturing influencers, supporting journalists and tracking performance along the way.

Leader Empathy: The leadership at your company plays a big role in earned media strategy. Leaders who deeply understand what their customers, prospects, employees and tribal members are thinking and feeling are well positioned to publish fresh content and insights that "earn" attention. Leaders who sell too hard and demand too much will likely fail in their earned media strategy, tactics and goals.

Influencer Tribe: You'll need to form relationships with influencers in your industry who have the clout, authority and fan base that align with your customers, prospects and fans. You'll need to carefully connect with these influencers by offering value, sharing insights and opinions, and opening yourself up to advancing **their** mission, stories and goals, **not yours.**

Journalist Tribe: The dynamic at most major publications has changed radically over the last few years. The army of full-time reporters, editors and journalists has been replaced by a battery of contributing journalists who are a mix of CEOs, thought leaders and freelance journalists, among others. You'll find many of these contributors cranking out posts on big publishers' blogs. Because they're not on staff, you'll need to track them down to build relationships before gently getting your name and brand in front of them in creative ways. Commenting on their posts helps them in a variety of ways. Pitching ideas to them for stories mildly related to your brand is another good tactic. Sharing stats, data and insights harvested from your database helps them "make a case" and connect your brand. But tread lightly. This is shaky ground, and selling them on how great your company is will not succeed.

Make the Case: Making a case for your company and brand to be in the spotlight goes well beyond your brand's accomplishments, new releases and other factors. Authors whose trust you want to earn must make a case for their stories with facts, data and research if they are to maintain credibility and influence with readers. Help those authors make the case by doing the research for them. If you think your conference is the best conference and worthy of the spotlight, research all the competitors and statistics about each of them, demonstrating why your conference is the best. Sure, they'll need to check your data, but you'll likely save them considerable time, creating a win-win.

Earned Media: Social Media

Earned media certainly includes all the mentions, shares and likes on your social accounts. The larger your social following and the activity and support of your fan base, the more likely you are to earn respect with influencers, authors and publications in a position to publish public stories supporting your brand. But remember this principle: You'll need to give love to receive love. You'll need to support your influencers, authors and publications with shares, likes, retweets and mentions if you expect them to reciprocate with support.

Reputation Management

You'll find many public review sites on the web; each of these constitutes an open invitation for your customers and prospects — ANYONE, really — to offer their thoughts and opinions on their experience with your products, services, company and brand. But that's just the beginning. Search marketing professionals use best practices to suppress negative reviews while highlighting better reviews to improve sentiment for the brand. Managing your reputation online is a marketing discipline that requires continual vigilance, but it can have a big impact on your bottom line.

Publication Spotlights

We highlighted the traditional public relations approach to cultivating media interest above. We're seeing today that companies are taking their own more direct approach, using the traditional tactics but in the new ways outlined.

Awards Shows

Exposing your brand and/or business at awards shows is another effective way to earn media. Winning an award helps to validate your excellence and leadership position in the marketplace. Leveraging that award in your social sphere can help your champions make a case for you to their fans, peers and executives. Awards also help make the case to your authors, influencers and publishers that you're worthy of support in the public.

Guest Blogging

Guest blogging, contributing blog posts to other blogs, is a highly effective tactic that can greatly expand your distribution, provide SEO benefits and increase your reach to new audiences. Search and find like-minded blogs with the authority, fan base, Alexa rating and clout that invite guest posts and are worthy of your time. Perform a search for these kinds of sites by entering terms such as "write for us" or "contribute to our blog." (Narrow your search to the niche you do business in.) The key to success is publishing quality content that appeals to the blogger's audience and drives traffic from search engines. If you take the time to research the topics already covered on the website, learn about the blogger's audience and optimize your content so it performs wonderfully, you will be asked to contribute more content.

Curation

Curation software like Scoop.it and Paper.li, Twitter Times, Rebel Mouse, Curata and Uberflip provides curation services that will help you gather the most appealing content, pick the winners, and publish the content on your own website, linking to the "full posts" on the original sites. The downside is that the content will be duplicative. You won't help your search engine marketing efforts and could, in fact, hurt them if you don't have enough "original" content published to balance the duplicate content. The upside is that your readers might very well enjoy your "rollup" and selection, view you as a consistent publisher of the best topics and stories, and keep returning for more of the same.

Influencers

Influencer marketing is the practice of getting leaders in your field or even celebrities to vouch for your brand and share your content.

Here are both a valuable resource featuring 30 ways to get serious about influencer marketing and an infographic featuring influencer marketing suggestions from 22 marketing leaders:

 Content Strategy MasterClass Resource Appendix: Links to an article by Barry Feldman and several other authors on Influencer Marketing.

News

"News coverage garners attention, fuels social amplification, builds brand credibility, and as it so happens, influences buyers," writes Sarah Skerik (author of "Driving Content Discovery") on the PR Newswire site. The online PR business is changing fast, but to give you an idea of what the most influential opinion shapers are doing to piggyback on the news, take a look at the Cision and Meltwater blogs and their industry coverage. One tactic is to ride the wave of big news stories by inserting your own insights, facts or data that might shift the conversation from the original news. Larry Kim, co-founder of WordStream, did just that in a response to Google's public stock offering.

Media Integration: The Three-Legged Stool

A solid content distribution plan needs to have contributions from paid, earned and owned media. Content marketers who lean too heavily on one to the detriment — or complete avoidance — of the others will struggle to find an audience for their content. Think of your plan as a stool: It stands on three legs.

As you ramp up — and amp up — your content promotion and distribution, don't lose sight of the need to integrate the paid, earned and owned approaches. Because these strategies complement each other, you're likely to extend your reach even more when you use them in combination.

Keep in mind: Each and every media placement should point back to your website or blog so you can capture traffic, leads and conversions. You'll want to publish original content to your central platform first, then direct paid and earned efforts back to your owned properties to drive engagement. Be open to perpetual experimentation. As you scale your content promotions, track your performance. Take costs and traffic measures into consideration, also how your efforts impact the achievement of specific goals. No formula is perfect. The ideal way to distribute content is to try a variety of strategies and refine where your money and time are spent based on the results.

CERTIFICATION REQUIREMENT:

In a Nutshell

Publish approved content from WriterAccess directly to one of your platforms including WordPress, Facebook, Twitter, HubSpot, Joomla, Movable Type, Drupal or more.

Exercise

Follow these steps to distribute content directly to platforms.

1. Click My Tools and Intergrations
2. Select one of your platforms for integration
3. Setup the integration with your credentials
4. Click Manage Workflow at WriterAccess
5. Select one of your orders for distribution
6. Select your platform
7. Follow the steps to distribute and publish

Certification Test

Then take the online Content Distribution test.

Facebook Ad

Below are two Facebook ads that may give you ideas for creating your own ad and earning your badge. Please review the Facebook Guidelines for Ads and use the testing engine located at the following address:

https://www.facebook.com/business/ads-guide/
https://www.facebook.com/ads/tools/

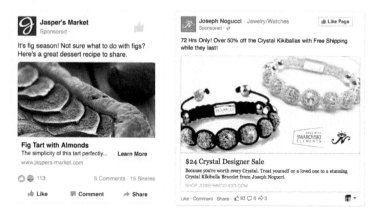

Helpful Tips

Explore BuzzSumo for ideas for snappy headlines for your blog post, tweets, posts and Facebook ad copy. Eye-catching headlines better grab readers orbiting at high speeds and boost clicks and shares in the social sphere.

Chapter 5:
Content Performance

Content Performance

Content Performance Overview

Content performance refers to the methodology and technology of measuring content marketing success, failure and/or impact on the business. You'll learn that there are many ways to track performance, ranging from conversion rates to user acquisition cost. But there also are many challenges, as you will see, such as how to correlate the revenue you achieve with particular content marketing campaigns. And pinpointing the influence of particular content assets is difficult, if not impossible. Stay tuned, because we'll have answers and unfold some of the mysteries.

These are some of the questions you will answer:

What are the Key Performance Indicators?
What are the tools to measure KPIs?
What are the tools to measure performance?
How long does it take to achieve performance goals?

One thing is for sure, when you develop the right content strategy and execute it with the right people, to the right audience, you'll achieve almost all of your content marketing performance goals.

You'll need to establish a culture of continual measurement, and that means daily, weekly, monthly, quarterly and yearly. Companies need to assess where they are now in the transformative process, and how long it will realistically take them to change the brand from sales plugger to publisher dialed into customers' wants and needs.

Setting the Benchmark

With all your content marketing goals, you'll want to take a snapshot of the current performance to establish a baseline for improvement. Take a look at the following ranking data example that helps to establish a baseline for search engine optimization goals.

Key Performance Goals

Companies seem to "want it all" when it comes to performance. But limiting focus to a few Key Performance Indicators (KPIs) is a better way to drive strategy and develop tactics to achieve company goals. Let's review the KPI list now, arranged by how difficult they are to achieve, so you can get the big picture first. Then you'll see some tips and advice on how to achieve these goals.

Easier to Achieve
1. Traffic
2. Conversion Enhancement
3. Long Tail Listing Positions
4. Leads
5. Time on Site

More Difficult to Achieve
6. Short Tail Listing Positions
7. Engagement: Likes, Shares, Comments
8. Links
9. Quality Leads
10. Referrals and Word Of Mouth
11. Channel Attribution
12. Email Open Rates

Very Difficult to Achieve
13. Churn Rate
14. Customer Acquisition Cost
15. Customer Lifetime Value
16. Content Asset Attribution

Ultimate Performance Goals
17. Brand Awareness
18. Revenue Growth

Easy Ways to Achieve Performance: You Can't Miss

1. Traffic

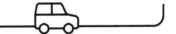

Creating a steady stream of content that appeals to readers and search engines should increase your overall traffic. The key is to create content for particular stages of the customer journey, especially if you have been ignoring the informational needs of customers and prospects at the various steps.

Expect three to six months to pass before you see the measurable traffic improvements that will be necessary to fine-tune your SEO strategy and achieve top listing in the search engines. To analyze an overall increase in traffic performance, you can correlate the amount of new content you publish in all your channels with your overall increases in traffic. Dive deeper by correlating the increases in particular channels with new content assets in those channels — for example, increases in blog traffic correlated with publishing frequency.

 Calculation: Visits are the total number of visits to your website, including repeat visits. Unique visits are the tally of all IP addresses that visit your website, which does not account for repeat visitors. Always use unique visits as the measure for the "traffic" or audience you're reaching.

 Free Tool: WordVison offers a free tool that each month displays your overall Google Analytics traffic and the number of posts you have on WordPress, Facebook and Twitter. You can see how much content you've published in each of those channels and how your overall traffic has been affected. Simply log on with a free trial and give it a whirl.

2. Conversion Enhancement

Conversion Rate Optimization is another goal that is relatively easy to achieve. Through adjustments to your landing page copy, graphics or layout, make it as painless as possible for visitors to respond to your Call to Action. Running simple A/B tests on your landing page will "move the needle" and deliver on the boost in performance you demand from your investment. We won't go too deeply into how to set up and run tests at this stage, but getting up and running is not too difficult. I've made this statement for many years: If you're not constantly testing your landing pages, you're living in the dinosaur age when it comes to marketing. Testing different headlines, creative, images and copy enables you to double or triple your conversion rates, with relative ease.

 Calculation: Conversion is defined as a visitor's taking action on your landing page. Depending on your industry and your offer, a response to your Call to Action can be downloading a white paper, signing up for a newsletter, watching a video, making a donation, or buying your product. Your conversion rate is the percentage of total visitors who click on your Call to Action.

 Newbie Tip: Give Visual Website Optimizer a whirl. It's easy to set up your first test and get it going so you can experience the power of testing.

3. Long Tail Listing Positions

Optimizing your content for the keywords that matter most is certainly a critical part of any content strategy. You'll need to select a balanced portfolio of both short- and long-tail keywords to reach your SERP goals. Short-tail keywords are more popular but make it more difficult to achieve a high ranking. Long-tail keywords are less popular but make it easier to achieve the rankings you desire.

 Calculation: Short-tail words are broad terms that searchers use when they are at the start of the customer journey. "Flat screen TV" is an example of a short tail expression that will produce a high volume of results. Long-tail words contain more detailed terms that searchers use as they move closer to purchase — for example, "42 inch Sony flat screen TV on sale." Choosing terms in both categories, as well as mid-tail terms, will give you the best chance for rankings that match visitor intent.

 Pro Tip: When you're selecting a core batch of keywords to target for SEO for a client, one great strategy is to balance the portfolio with one third long-tail keywords, one third short-tail keywords and one third "Low Hanging Fruit." Low Hanging Fruit, described in Chapter 1, are keywords for which the client's website already occupies a position between 11 and 100. With this knowledge, you will be in a position to build content and internal links around those LHF keywords to move the site to a position from 1 to 10 on page 1 of the results. The site's newfound higher visibility will help to increase its traffic flow.

4. Leads

A lead can be anyone who has raised a hand in response to an offer or who has expressed interest in your content. Generating leads should follow from a solid content strategy and investment in content marketing. Increasing your content spend will generate more leads, especially if you aim that spend to reach new customers orbiting at high speeds. But more leads alone are not necessarily going to help you achieve your revenue goals. There's a tip below that should help you fine-tune your strategy as you grow your overall lead base, something that is not too terribly difficult to achieve.

 Calculation: Lead generation relies on source attribution. You will need to know where each lead is coming from in order to determine which content assets are engaging readers and which are missing the mark. Thus, you will want to use a unique tracking code for each piece of content. Make sure goals are set up properly in Google Analytics for each campaign. And make sure each lead in your CRM is tagged with its source.

 Pro Tip: Create a buyer persona for "bad leads" that you do not want to bring into your lead funnel. Distinguish between a good and bad lead, with reference to as many characteristics of a bad lead as possible. In compiling your bad lead persona, talk to sales reps who manage leads and ask them whom they "don't want to talk to." Use that information to differentiate good leads from great leads. Look at sources for your best leads, determine which content assets interest your best leads and your worst, and align your marketing message accordingly.

5. Time on Site

HubSpot reports that 55 percent of visitors spend 15 seconds or less on a website. Take a look at your analytics and see how you stack up. Your best content will have more "stickiness" with readers, customers and fans. Dive into your Google Analytics and take a look at overall time on page for your website, and the times for individual pages. The more great content you publish, the more time your readers and fans will spend on your site.

Bounce rate also should be measured and tracked. High bounce rates are interpreted by search engines as a sign of low-quality content that doesn't engage.

 Calculation: Time on Site is the average time all visitors spend on a website. Time on Page is the average time each visitor spends on a particular page. Bounce rate is the percentage of single page visits to your website.

 Pro Tip: Take a look at the most "sticky" page on your website, and analyze the content type, topic and phase of the customer journey. See if that top-performing page led to sales, with attribution back to its sticky content assets.

More Difficult Ways to Achieve Performance: Go for It!

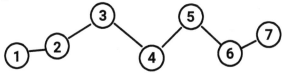

6. Short-tail Listing Positions

If you want to secure top listings for the most popular keywords, the bar is set higher. The competition for short-tail keywords is fierce, so you'll have to bring your "A" game. You'll need outstanding content on your website, optimized for those keywords, PLUS links from authoritative websites to those optimized pages. Direct links from websites with authority seem to be the driver for search marketing success. Use internal links to cross-pollinate your content. Social shares also figure in to the ranking algorithm, according to many SEO professionals.

 Pro Tip: Monitor performance of different groups of keywords, especially competitive short-tail terms. Avoid purchasing links, as that continues to be a black hat practice. Instead, amplify your best content in the social sphere to improve visibility, potential linking and shares.

7. Engagement: Likes, Shares, Comments

In a groundbreaking content analysis, BuzzSumo teamed up with Moz to study the shares and links of more than a million articles. Their goal was to analyze the correlation of shares and links, to understand the nature of content that attracts both shares and links, and to identify formats that get relatively more shares or links.

BuzzSumo later partnered with Majestic to identify how marketers could improve their content to generate more engagement. The results showed five distinct content types that have the potential to perform with the highest number of likes, shares and links from authoritative websites:

1. Authoritative content that answers popular questions
2. Strong opinion posts and political posts
3. Researched content supporting counterintuitive thinking
4. Leveraged content on trending topics
5. Authoritative news about new products, services or developments

Tracking the content assets you publish in terms of likes, shares and links is just the beginning when it comes to measuring content engagement. Each of your publishing channels can be analyzed for engagement as well; that includes Facebook, Twitter, LinkedIn and other social channels. Analyzing content type in conjunction with performance also helps to map out engagement in a unique way.

Pro Tip: Try to fit your top-performing content into these five BuzzSumo categories. Discover which are performing better and resonating with your customers and prospects. Take things one step further to see how much revenue you can attribute to a single download, view or engagement with these top performers. Learn from the engagement performance data what's working, and what's not.

Content Strategy MasterClass Resource Appendix: Links to both Buzz Sumo and Moz sharing insights on the analysis.

8. Links

We've established that increasing the number of inbound links to your website will boost your authority and improve your listing positions on the search engine results pages. But when it comes to links, quality trumps quantity. You need high-quality links from authoritative websites. When other sites link to particular pages on your website that feature popular content that offers information, answers, insights and/or solutions for readers, this factors into Google's algorithm. If you're creating engaging content and amplifying it to catch readers with the right information at the right time, you'll grow your link popularity. Link performance is fairly easy to track but, depending on the quality of your content, more difficult to achieve.

 Pro Tip: Quickly view all your inbound links using Spyfu, SEMRUSH, MOZ or Majestic and see how you stack up with the competition.

9. Quality Leads

Generating the best leads takes time and analysis. Analyzing the lifetime value of customers who engage with content marketing campaigns is but one way to measure the quality of leads. It shouldn't end there. Marketing, sales and customer service need to work together to assess the quality of leads on more than one level. For example, from a customer service standpoint, customers who absorb more time and expense may spend more, but have less value to the business. This points out the importance of measuring the quality of leads in a variety of ways, and letting the data determine what kind of content will boost quality based on your content strategy and investment.

 Pro Tip: Take the time to craft buyer personas, using demographic information and input from sales, customer success and marketing team members to help writers create the type of content that will drive the highest quality leads.

10. Referrals and Word of Mouth

A helpful tool for tracking potential word-of-mouth recommendations from customers is the Net Promoter Score (NPS). Improvement in your customers' Net Promoter Scores is a gauge of success and can be tracked. If you don't currently use NPS, we strongly recommend you give it a go. Customers answer one single question: On a scale of 1 to 10, how likely are you to recommend our products or services to others?

Growth in referrals should also be tracked. A customer referred to you by a neutral third party with an honest recommendation should spend more, faster. And by creating special referral campaigns and content centered on referrals, you can help drive more revenue, and help make the case for more content marketing spend.

 Pro Tip: Take a look at the lifetime spend of customers who were "recommended" and tracked through your referral program, and compare it with the lifetime spend of customers from other sources. If you find better results from referrals, and you've influenced those referrals through content strategy and content marketing campaigns, you'll be in a position to secure more funding for those efforts.

11. Channel Attribution

As part of your content strategy, you'll likely be distributing that content to multiple channels: Facebook, Twitter, LinkedIn, blogs and other sources of promotion. Analyze the content channels that drive traffic to your website. Track that traffic so that you can start attributing growth and performance improvement by channel. Evaluating your traffic by source can reveal the relative strengths and weaknesses of your social media, SEO, email and other forms of distribution and promotion.

Pro Tip: Dive into your Google Analytics account and take a look at how much traffic is being directed to your website from channels where you regularly publish content. Using an overlay or comparison chart, map out traffic, conversion and revenue growth by channel over select periods of time, and correlate with increases in publishing frequency or engagement over the same periods of time.

12. Email Open Rates

Open rate is the percentage of recipients who open an email. Rates vary greatly depending on the quality of your content and engagement with your subscribers. The average open rate falls around 2 percent, although high-performing email distribution lists can achieve 10 percent and above.

 Pro Tip: Bring on the ABC's when it comes to email marketing: Always Be Conversion rate testing your headlines to boost open rates. See which terms, questions, brand names or other keywords result in higher open rates.

Very Difficult to Achieve: Where There's a Will ...

13. Churn Rate

Churn rate is the proportion of customers who leave your business during a given period of time because of dissatisfaction, competitive disadvantage, or reasons related to the customer life cycle. Lowering churn rate is a difficult proposition, but not beyond your ability to achieve if you are diligent about investing in content for existing customers.

According to Gartner, it costs five times as much to attract a new customer as it does to keep an existing customer. John Daly, author of Pricing for Profitability, contends the cost is times ten. Investing in content obviously is a must. It can pay big dividends by decreasing churn and increasing revenue. Establish an overall baseline churn rate for all customers before and after your content plan rollout, and track improvements and/or challenges along the way.

 Calculation: For SaaS models, calculate revenue churn by taking the amount of recurring revenue LOST in a period divided by the total revenue at the beginning of the period. To calculate your content marketing investment's impact on churn rate, focus on customer lifetime value (below) and analyze the impact of content assets on customer revenue and spend.

 Pro Tip: As you develop your content plan, reach out to existing customers and learn the types of content assets and topics that offer value, build loyalty and propel customers to stay with you for the long haul. Of course, it's not your customers' job to develop your content plan. You'll do that by experimenting with a wide range of content assets, tracking their performance through their impact — both positive and negative — on churn rates and lifetime value.

14. Customer Acquisition Cost

To scale your content marketing budgets upward, you'll need to analyze the investments needed to "acquire" a new customer and the cost for that acquisition.

 Calculation: To calculate CAC for your paid advertising on a particular channel, simply divide the total spend on that channel for a set period of time by the number of "conversions" for trials and/or purchases of your product or service during that same period. To calculate overall CAC for content marketing, we recommend you use the same formula. To achieve a more meaningful figure, you may want to parse out the fixed costs of content marketing such as content planning and strategy, focusing only on the cost to create and optimize content. Regardless of whether you calculate CAC for a given channel or overall, be consistent with the methodology and your tracking, so you can pinpoint success and failure along the way.

 Content Strategy MasterClass Resource Appendix: Link to an article by Kiss Metrics about Customer Acquisition Cost.

15. Customer Lifetime Value

Calculate customer lifetime value by using historic data from existing customers to help predict the gross profit or net profit of new customers. Essentially, CLV is the present value of future cash flows of customers during their "lifetime" with the business. Knowing CLV will help you keep your spend to acquire new customers within reasonable bounds.

 Calculation: To calculate CAC, simply divide the average total revenue generated by all customers, by the total spend or "term" with the business.

 Pro Tip: Your investment in content assets supporting the customer service team should improve Net Promoter Score and customer satisfaction.

16. Content Asset Attribution

Tracking the impact of a single content asset can be challenging. To give yourself a fighting chance of success, you first need to pull some general analytics information from each of your channels to assess how certain content assets are performing. Here's a quick summary of metrics you can access in a few channels:

- LinkedIn metrics show individual post views and engagement data, along with comments stats for your posts.
- Twitter metrics show the number of tweets, retweets,

mentions, responses and direct messages.

- Facebook metrics show the number of post views, comments and shares for each post.
- Email shares can be tracked through CMS platforms such as HubSpot, Wordpress and Pardot.

Lead generation is the biggest challenge for 61 percent of B2B marketers, according to Content Marketing Institute. It's likely that most of your larger content assets will be intended to drive leads.

 Calculation: Track the engagement of every content asset you publish, including shares, comments, tweets and retweets. Also, track the lead generation for each content asset you publish and promote. Analyze the visitor-to-lead conversion rates for individual content assets, and the lifetime value of customers who downloaded content assets in comparison with customers who did not engage with those same content assets.

 Pro Tip: BuzzSumo tracks the most popular content assets being published on the web, using an SaaS model called Majestic to provide a full analysis of the number of shares, tweets, retweets and link popularity.

Ultimate Performance Goals: Grabbing the Brass Ring

17. Brand Awareness

To be the top-of-mind brand for the products and services you sell is the ultimate marketing goal. But earning that authoritative status takes a lot of work and time. And even once you've earned it, you may not always be credited for it, because marketing professionals are somewhat divided on how brand awareness can and should be measured.

The old school of thought is that one of the strongest drivers motivating decisions to buy is the consumer's recall of the product, logo and even tagline of the business, supported by celebrity endorsement and traditional mass marketing. Under this school of thought, brand awareness is typically measured through focus group testing, surveys and other more traditional, tedious tasks.

The newer school of thought looks more closely at website traffic and search volume for branded keywords, products and the brand name. It also takes into consideration "direct" traffic from customers and prospects — those who land directly on the business page without going through the search results. Social listening is a much better way to look at brand awareness, eliminating surveys and response bias.

The bottom line is that if your business is doing "good things," cranking out content that engages customers and gets passed around, you'll be in a position to measure brand awareness in a variety of meaningful ways.

18. Revenue Growth

Revenue growth is what we all want to see from any investment, especially in content marketing, which can be more difficult to measure and track. To understand the true ROI of content marketing, we need to look at the customer experience throughout the journey, well beyond the conversion and sale.

At the beginning of the customer journey, in the discovery stage, the average time it takes for a customer to be "ready to purchase" varies considerably from business to business. Once you establish a baseline time frame moving forward from the discovery stage and build out your content marketing campaigns to engage at that stage, any shortening of the time line can directly affect revenue in a positive way.

As customers deepen their relationship with your company and proceed through the customer journey, the opportunity for revenue growth expands even more. In the later stages of the journey, online reviews and personal referrals come into play. More than 88 percent of customers say they trust online reviews as much as they do personal referrals. Thus, growing revenue depends on continued investment in high-quality content at these later stages in the journey, fostering growth through referrals, reviews and word of mouth marketing.

Creating Great Content Requires Powerful Tools

The marketplace contains numerous content creation and content marketing tools. These tools include platforms for finding writers, creating graphics, tracking performance and more. Take a look at my book "Top 139 Content Marketing Tools" and find the tools that are best for you and your goals.

In a Nutshell

With your domain(s) and keywords now loaded into WriterAccess, you can dive into Analytics Reports to surface with a better understanding of how well your content is performing, and how well it's optimized for readers and the search engines.

Exercise

Follow these steps for content performance assessment.

1. Click My Tools and Analytics
2. Click Content Analytics and Noodle with Settings and Filters
3. Click Keyword Analytics and Noodle with Settings and Filters
4. Click Analytics Report and Download/Email Report
5. Click Tool Setup Report Logo and Add Your Logo

Certification Test

Then take the online Content Performance Test

About WriterAccess Content Analytics

WriterAccess content analytics is free software offered to all customers that tracks how much content you're publishing on WordPress, Facebook and Twitter, and how well the content is optimized and performing in the search engines. The integrations with WordPress, Facebook, Twitter, SpyFu, Bit.ly and Google Analytics pull in all the data directly from their platforms. After you set up the integrations, which takes just a few minutes, the technology runs around the clock, keeping track and reporting back the changes and updates.

The Keyword Analytics report uses SpyFu intergration to harvest monthly SERP(Search Engine Result Position) rankings at Google and Bing/Yahoo, tracking monthly search engine listing positions for each keyword phrase. The variations each month are also tracked, so you can pinpoint the rising and falling keywords to adjust optimization strategy.

The Content Analytics displays how many keywords are used in any of the content you're publishing, along with Bit.ly clicks, giving you more indicators for betterment of confirmation for success.

Helpful Tip

Once you set up the integrations on WriterAccess and load your keywords, the software will start running, but it will not show you any data until the first day of the following month. Simply log in and click on Reports to review and download your first report after the first day of the following month.

Chapter 6:
Content Management

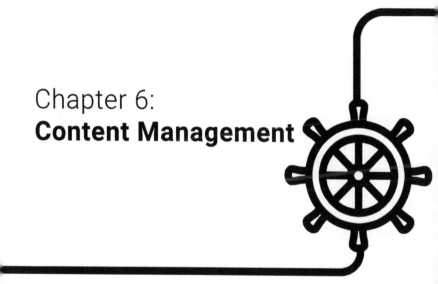

Content Management

Content Management Overview

Managing, polishing and publishing a steady stream of high-quality content — propelled through the five phases of planning, creation, optimization, distribution and performance — is the mission of a content strategist. The process, people and team are the three pillars that determine success or failure, namely, getting the right person (or people) with the right skills doing the right things, every minute of every day.

In this chapter, we'll cover the game plan for content management that keeps the content engine going and flowing. We'll define the products that need to be produced, the people who need to be put in place, and the team dynamic required to keep the content marketing engine chugging. Content marketing, after all, is a team sport involving lots of moving parts. Depending on the size of your organization, those parts may include a writer (or writers), editor, designer, SEO specialist and project manager. We'll examine the roles of these individual contributors and compare three different teams based on size, content goals and budget. And we'll offer a special shout-out to the MVP — who else but the content strategist, of course!

I. Content Products   III. The Team
II. The Players   IV. MVP: Content Strategist

Workflow Tools

When it comes to content management, you need the latest tools to help manage people, implement process and track the workflow. The quantity of content you create, the size of your staff and the nature of your infrastructure will determine the workflow tools you select.

Below is a list of the most popular workflow tools recommended by our speakers at the Content Marketing Conference:

Basecamp	Marketing MO
Content Analysis Tool	NewsCred
Curation Soft	Opal
DivvyHQ	Ripenn
Gather Content	ScribbleLive
Huddle	Slickplan
Jumpchart	Wrike
Kapost	

Content Strategy Masterclass Resource Appendix: Link to my book "Top 139 Content Marketing Tools" offering descriptions, pros and cons.

Editorial Calendar

If you're serious about content and producing enough of it to impact your revenue, you'll need an editorial calendar where you can post content asset types, topics, deadlines and publishing targets. Next-gen editorial calendars will go even further by assisting all your team members to keep on top of edits, revision, feedback, performance and even mapping to the customer journey, personas and SEO strategy.

Content Strategy Masterclass Resource Appendix: Explore a free Content Planning Tool and Editorial Calendar Tool.

I. CONTENT PRODUCTS

Content products are my name for the key documents that drive content strategy and help unite all your team members behind the goals and strategy for success. Let's walk through each product quickly, with some quick instructions as to how they're developed and created for guidance.

1. Keyword Map
2. Customer Journey
3. Buyer Personas
4. Creative Briefs
5. Website Audit
6. Content Audit

1. Keyword Map

Optimizing content for readers and search engines starts by researching and selecting the best keywords and organizing those keywords into topic groups that help writers drive performance. Here's the step-by-step process:

- Research all the keywords driving organic and paid traffic to your competitors and authority websites in your industry. You'll quickly find 10K to 100K keywords, which can become the starting point for analysis.
- Start sorting and grouping keywords by name, PPC price, ranking difficulty, current rankings for you and your competition, and other comparables. All this is possible with the data you pull using tools like SpyFu, Moz and others.
- Weed out the duplicates and find the terms that make sense to target for both search engines and reader appeal. Find keywords that are long-, mid-, and short-tail in terms of

ranking difficulty.

- Finally, you'll select anywhere from 100 to 1,000 keywords to target, depending on how much content budget you have and your goals for publishing. You'll group these keywords into categories or keyword silos that are aligned with content topics you plan to write about.

2. Customer Journey

By mapping out the customer's journey and documenting what your prospects and customers are experiencing on their journey, you can get the right content asset in front of the right people at the right time. This tool does all that, helping content creators understand the wants and needs of customers at every stage of their journey. The content produced in response to those wants and needs will help turn browsers into believers, believers into buyers, and buyers into word-of-mouth marketers who will start the cycle all over again. To map a customer journey:

- Host several meetings with both customers and representatives from marketing, sales, customer success and any other departments with front-line experience working with customers.
- Learn and document what customers are thinking and feeling at various stages of the journey: Discover, Investigate, Consider, Trial, Purchase, Perceive, Connect and Share.
- Another goal is to learn and document the current content assets or channels that address those customer thoughts, feelings and concerns, and how those content assets are performing in terms of engagement, downloads and impact on sales.
- The final step is to recommend topics for blog posts, articles and other content assets that might engage customers or prospects at a particular stage of the journey.

3. Buyer Personas

Without a deep understanding of who your customers are, marketing fails in many ways. Highlighting the characteristics and distinctions of multiple personas helps writers and marketers personalize content assets for different buyers, increasing engagement, conversion and performance. The more data you can provide from your customer database, the more accurate the buyer personas will be; that, in turn, will boost content performance. To properly develop customer personas:

- You'll need data revealing demographics, location, spending habits, skills and proficiency, pain points and objectives, and you'll need to champion the characteristics of the best customers.
- The number of personas you develop will depend on the diversity of your products, services and customer base.
- Three is a good number to help parse out the distinctions among different groups of customers and to provide enough directions in which to aim content creation.
- You'll find lots of free samples online, so do take a look.

4. Creative Brief

Creative brief help writers and designers (creatives) understand the goals for projects, documenting the scope of the project and target audience, including particular buyer personas. Creatives often refer back to the creative brief to refresh and guide the creative process to deliver on goals for engagement, connection and performance. The brief defines the project, purpose, goals, situation, complexity and alternative solutions along with other variables like tone, style and execution strategy recommended for success.

5. Website Audit

A thorough analysis of your website's visibility to search engines will offer a deep understanding of any obstacles standing in the way of drawing more traffic or more sales. This product combines an automated website audit tool with a hand-review of your website analytics reports to uncover roadblocks and opportunities to improve performance. To conduct a website audit:

- Select your favorite website audit report software like SpyFu or Moz.
- Run a report to quickly pinpoint the roadblocks.
- Fix any and all problems with your code, technology or performance issues.
- Engage with your Google Analytics and Google webmaster tools.
- Fix any and all code, technology or performance challenge issues.
- Run monthly reports to confirm that all problems have been fixed.

6. Content Audit

To win the war of words on the web, you need to know how your content stacks up with the competition in terms of quality, quantity, publishing frequency and performance. Only then can you craft a content strategy to come off victorious. This product offers the answers through research that compares your content with your competition, helping you capture mind share and market share in the search engines. To perform a content audit:

- Select your favorite competitive research software like SpyFu or Moz.
- Identify your current market share vs. the competition.
- Document all your content assets' types, quantity and

publishing frequency.
- Do the same for your competition.
- Roll all the data up into the Content Audit Report.
- Compare how you stack up with the competition.

II. THE PLAYERS

Let's take a look at the dream team that is on every content strategist's love list. Kapost, maker of a content marketing platform for large companies, asked more than 500 marketers how many people at their companies are assigned to support content marketing. More than 90 percent of respondents said 10 or fewer. The most common team size was two to five members. Fewer than 20 percent of content marketing teams comprise six or more people.

Our view is that the dream team for any company spending $500,000 or more on content marketing ideally should include seven members, each with a specific area of expertise. Working together, this gang of seven can help the company meet its content marketing goals:

1. Content Strategist
2. Writer
3. Optimizer
4. Designer
5. Analyst
6. Editor
7. Digital Marketing Manager

Even if your business isn't in a position to accommodate all these players on your team, we want you to know who they are and what they could and would do to keep your content and your performance flowing. We'll review these roles and goals and discuss the flex for any business and budget size that will deliver the performance you demand from your content marketing investment.

1. Content Strategist

The content strategist plays the most important role on the team. Content strategists have a passion for developing strategic plans that achieve specific marketing goals. They actively use software tools for keyword research, content curation, competitive research, performance analysis, strategic planning and other content marketing research. Depending on marketing goals, complexity of the work and budget, content strategists are likely to have a diverse set of skills and experience, including writing, editing, content planning and media buying (content amplification). The key to their success lies in resources — a network or platform of freelance writers, editors, designers and other professionals who can help create the content assets required for success.

Content Strategist Skills Checklist:

> Content Marketing Wizardry
> Keyword Research
> Content Curation
> Competitive Research
> Content Plan Creation
> Freelancer Management
> Writing/Editing
> Content Workflow Management
> Performance Measurement
> Content Management Software and Tools

2. Writer

Companies may need various types of writers, depending on their industry, their audience and the content assets they're creating. Copywriters, tech writers, article writers, instructional writers and other writing specialists usually come with specific skill sets. It's rare to find an individual who can write fluently and knowledgably in all these roles.

Smaller teams typically outsource content to screened, proven professionals sourced from writer networks like WriterAccess, Scripted, Textbroker and others. Larger companies and teams, on the other hand, often have in-house writers to produce their content. No matter how you create your content, your writer must have the skills, experience and expertise to create content that hits the goals.

Characteristics of great writers:

- Passionate about the topic
- Master of digital media
- Understand the paradox of choice
- Appeal to different readers
- Know how to shape perception
- Know how to find new meaning
- Understand the power of storytelling
- Take creative risks
- Sensational style flexors

This checklist was developed over years of working with hundreds and thousands of writers at WriterAccess. Great writers possess many of the qualities on this list, but none have them all. Use the list as a guide when evaluating writers on your team and refer back to Chapter 2 for a deeper explanation of each characteristic.

Training and Certification

At WriterAccess, writers apply for certification badges that promote their skills and proficiency. These badges, our writer test, and samples submitted by writers all help customers to pinpoint the skills and proficiencies they are seeking. While certification isn't necessary for a skilled writer, certification courses can improve skills and boost performance and are one other clue that a writer is a committed professional.

 Content Strategy Masterclass Resource Appendix: Links to 10+ certification organizations for writers.

3. Optimizer

Content optimizers turbocharge the performance of all the content that's created, published and produced. The core responsibility of the optimization specialist is improving conversion rates. Optimization specialists appreciate that many different elements can contribute to conversion, so they constantly test content and design combinations, looking for key contributors to sales.

Search engine optimization, while perhaps best known, is only one kind of optimization practiced by specialists. Other types of optimization were covered in detail in Chapter 3. Optimization of all kinds requires the application of both technology and methodology for success. Specialists understand and practice the art and science of optimization, always learning along the way.

The most experienced optimization professionals have worked in larger companies with larger budgets. They have had the luxury of being able to conduct a bigger "sampling" of tests and experiments that help identify which optimization practices work and which do not work.

Optimization Specialist Skills Checklist:

- Search Engine Optimization
- Content Optimization
- Multi-Channel Distribution
- Link Building
- Landing Page Optimization
- Testing Methodology
- Testing Software
- Multivariate Testing
- Conversion Path Tuning
- Website Content Management System

It's a given that we want all the content we publish to drive free organic traffic from search engines. In Chapter 3, we discussed the optimization process in detail. As a refresher, remember that for your website to rank higher in search engine results, your content must feature keywords and keyword phrases that are relevant to that content.

4. Designer

In this new age of information clutter, standing out from the pack is challenging. More so than ever, design and designers play a critical role in differentiating products and services. The role of the designer is not simply to design a landing page, website or content asset. Design starts with a deep understanding of the customer journey, which leads organically to the design of the brand. Designers bring the brand's story to life, making it enchanting and unforgettable.

In recent years, neuroscience and neuromarketing have had a deep influence on design by focusing attention on the dominant emotional component of purchasing decisions. Designers influenced by this new wave of "human-centered" design try to reach customers emotionally at each touch point of the journey.

Designers often begin their process by creating a storyboard that visualizes the journey. Each touch point in the customer journey is illustrated in sequence. The elements of sight, sound, motion and emotion appear in the storyboard, revealing what the customer is thinking and feeling at each stage.

Designer Skills Checklist:

Branding
Storytelling
Storyboarding
Graphic Design
Multi-Channel Marketing
A/B Testing
Email Formats
Website Creation Tools (WordPress, Squarespace, etc.)
Typography
Illustration
Animation
User Experience

Creating a Brand Language

Once storyboarding is complete and the customer journey has been documented and visualized, designers establish a brand "language" that effectively communicates the brand's distinction. That language, which can be visual, written or both, is often referred to as the "look and feel" of the brand. The language must align with the business's vision and its commitment to make customers' lives smarter and better.

Years ago, while working for Hill Holliday, I learned much about how to motivate consumers throughout the buying process. I saw that the architecture of how a brand and product should make a customer "feel" extended well beyond marketing, through product design, sales, customer service and employee advocacy. Designers back in those days did not have the tools or resources they have now. But their methodology was spot on, extending well beyond a single campaign.

Michael Benes, an award-winning designer and brand guru, described it like this: When consumers flip through a magazine, the decision as to whether they will stop on any given page is made in milliseconds, and it is based on the design and images. If you are very lucky, they will read the headline, maybe even the copy, and perhaps connect with your brand on some level. But for marketing magic to happen, the story needs to stay with them long after they put the magazine away. Design is the first connection that starts the customer journey.

5. Analyst

Marketing analysts play an important role on the team, making sure all your marketing dollars and time allotments are maximizing the investment. Crunching big data to analyze that investment is part of the mix, but of greater importance is presenting that data in a way that helps drive decisions. If your content marketing budgets are $500,000 or more, a full-time marketing analyst might pay big dividends.

Marketing Analyst Skills Checklist:

Big Data Research
Big Data Reporting and
  Presentation
Marketing Automation
Performance Analysis
Content Attribution

Content Analytics
Conversion Analytics
Lead Scoring
Marketing Spend Analysis
Marketing ROI Analysis

The devil is in the details. Just ask any marketing analyst or the Van Halen production team. Van Halen requested "No brown M&Ms

in the dressing room" in its 1982 World Tour contract rider. This has often been described as an outlandish demand of pampered rock stars. The group has said the M&M provision was actually included to make sure that promoters had read the rider. If brown M&Ms were in the backstage candy bowl, the Van Halen team knew that more important aspects of a performance — safety, lighting, staging, security, ticketing — may have been overlooked. Likewise, your customers will test your attention to detail, which is where marketing analysis enters the picture. Rise to the occasion. Don't miss the opportunity.

6. Editor

A content editor is responsible for reviewing content marketing materials to ensure the highest quality deliverables. This person must have a gift for polishing copy and editing content to perfection, along with a basic understanding of search engine optimization, keyword research and social media, and be passionate about a content marketing career.

Content Editor Skills Checklist:

- Written and verbal communication skills
- Grammar and syntax skills
- In-depth knowledge of domain
- Attention to detail
- Ability to ensure high-quality, error-free work
- Understanding of digital format
- Ability to effectively manage workload
- Knowledge of target audience

7. Digital Marketing Manager

A digital marketing manager is a navigator of the digital space who knows how to amplify content assets and propel lead generation and sales. The digital marketing manager is responsible for the lead gen machine, ratcheting up brand awareness through digital ad campaigns and social media, cohesive product launch plans, and enhanced brand perception in cyberspace.

Digital Marketing Manager Checklist:

- Passion for inbound marketing, lead gen, social media marketing, SEO, events and content creation
- Comprehensive knowledge of the major publishing, social and distribution channels
- Data-driven approach and thirst for answers from the latest performance tools
- Knowledge of Search Engine Marketing (SEM)
- Experience with both A/B and multivariant testing on a small and large scale
- Well-versed in email marketing strategy, tactics and technology
- In tune with the latest mobile marketing strategy and tactics to reach new customers
- Competitive intelligence always top of mind, tracking market share and mindshare data
- In tune with the latest market trends, competition, customer needs and challenges

Team Manager

Your content marketing budget, workflow process and team infrastructure must all be carefully defined and aligned with your goals. As you've learned throughout this workbook, completion of many content marketing tasks is required for success. The digital marketing manager builds the team, sets the budget and lines up the season.

III. CONTENT MARKETING IS A TEAM SPORT

Your budget for content marketing has a lot to do with the size of the team and the processes you need to have in place to make content marketing perform to your goals. We'll walk through three different team sizes, discussing how each team "gets it done" in content marketing. Keep in mind that smaller companies have smaller budgets and may require only one or two full-time staff members to achieve goals. Larger teams with larger budgets will produce more content assets and expect more performance from the investments, requiring more team members for success.

	Tennis	Basketball	Football
Numbers of Players on the Team	**1 -2**	**3-5**	**10+**
Content Marketing Budget/Year	$60,000	$120,000+	$250,000+
Content Amplification Budget/Year	**$10,000**	**$30,000**	**$100,000**

Tennis: A Small Team

Team Size: 1–2

Content Strategist
Digital Marketing Manager

One or two key players can drive content marketing with the help of freelance content creators. A strong digital marketing manager with deep experience in industry marketing channels and databases will push out content and bring in leads. The larger the budget for a one- or two-person operation, the greater is the strain that will be placed on the team.

A tennis-sized team should develop simple content plans with keyword research to help aim the strategy in the right direction. It must test and prove marketing channels before "going big." Most importantly, both team members need to think strategically, gathering ideas, developing stories and learning what works and what does not work, to amplify the winning content assets to increase traffic, leads and conversions.

Tennis: Skills and Goals

One or two team members can accomplish many of the core tasks required for content marketing success. With only two people in our marketing department, WriterAccess zoomed from 100 to 22,000 customers. Sure, it helped to be able to outsource lots of work to hundreds of freelance writers, editors and even content strategists. But we produced all of the monthly content marketing goals and tracked all the monthly KPIs listed here, along with most of the monthly KPIs you'll find next on the more comfortably staffed basketball team.

Core Skills	Monthly KPIs	Monthly Content Goals
Writing	**Organic Traffic**	**10 to 60 Blog Posts**
Editing	Organic Conversion Rate	1 to 2 Long-Form Articles
Topic Ideation	**PPC Traffic**	**1 e-Newsletter**
Freelancer Management	PPC Conversion Rate	1 Email Promotion
SEO Optimization	**Downloads**	**Leads for 1 or 2 Sales Reps**
Industry Marketing	Subscriptions	
Channels	**User Acquisition Cost**	
Performance Tools		
Workflow Management		

Basketball: A Medium-Size Team

Team Size: 4–5

Digital Marketing Manager
Content Strategist
Optimizer/Analyst
Writer/Copywriter
Designer

Larger companies that have decided to go big with content marketing will need more players doing more tasks to help exceed performance goals. This team of four or five members can crank out the work and drive revenue goals. They can divide, conquer and perform with particular skills and expertise required for success.

The more complicated your sales and marketing funnel is, the more challenging it is to strip it down and make it simple. The best teams understand the power of simplicity in content creation, design and user experience development. Team management success depends largely on having set expectations for each team member and on monitoring the team's work weekly, inspecting the individual, department and company KPIs that must be achieved to maximize return on investment in both team members and content marketing spend.

Basketball: Skills and Goals

Take one look at the KPIs and monthly content goals for the basketball team, and you'll see the increase in work and time that is required to keep content flowing and performance going month after month at a larger enterprise. The number of assets produced each month greatly increases, fueling a goal of leads that will satisfy five to 10 sales reps.

Core Skills	Monthly KPIs	Monthly Content Goals
All Tennis Skills	All Tennis KPIs	All the Tennis Goals
PLUS	PLUS	PLUS
Multi-Channel Distribution	Trade Show Conversions	News/Evergreen Blog Posts
Social Engagement	A/B Testing Conversions	Infographics
Content Strategy	Time On Page	White Papers
AB Testing	Customer Touch Points	Press Releases
Storytelling vs. Selling	Customer Lifetime Value	Leads for 5 to 10 Sales Reps

Football: A Larger Team

Team Size: 10+

Chief Marketing Officer
Content Strategist
Writer(s)
Editor
Optimization Specialist
Landing Page Testing Specialist
Marketing Analyst
Lead Gen Specialist
Research Specialist
Email Marketing Specialist
Designer(s)
Illustrator
Animator
Videographer

Companies with bigger content marketing goals and performance objectives need to scale the team to meet these goals. These companies have a longer, more complex customer journey. Their content needs run the gamut across owned, earned and paid channels. This echelon of content marketing requires a team of 10 or more players with higher-level skills and specialist expertise. The more complicated your sales and marketing funnel is, the more challenging it will be to create, optimize, distribute and manage content and user experience development, and to maximize the return on investment of both team members and content marketing spend.

Football: Skills and Goals

The KPIs and monthly content goals for this company require a football-sized squad of marketers. The number of assets produced each month greatly increases, as the company moves into thought leadership and influencer marketing to reach and engage customers. Content marketing teams the size of a football team have more players, but are under more pressure to deliver to hungry sales reps leads that drive revenue and goals.

Core Skills	Monthly KPIs	Monthly Content Goals
All Tennis Skills	All Tennis KPIs	All the Tennis Goals
All Basketball Skills	**All Basketball KPIs**	**All the Basketball Goals**
PLUS	PLUS	PLUS
Social Engagement	**Decrease User Acquisition Cost**	**Webinars**
Multivariate Testing	Increase Reach	Speaking Gigs
Revenue Optimization	**Conversion Rates**	**Guest Blogging**
Community Building	NPS (Net Promoter Score)	Book Publishing
Neuromarketing Science	**Content Amplification Budget**	**Awards**
Branding and Design		Press
Thought Leadership		**Videos**

IV. MVP: Content Strategist

Content strategists are the MVPs and champions of content marketing. Here's a checklist of characteristics of the cream of the crop:

- Writes every day to continually refine his or her skills
- Demonstrated ability to create content that inspires, educates and performs
- Solid online identity and active in social media sphere
- Multi-dimensional marketer who uses the latest conversion tactics
- Fresh portfolio of content campaigns that achieved remarkable results
- In tune with the latest content marketing and strategy trends, tactics and news
- Capable of working with and motivating all team members to exceed goals

The Many Roles of an MVP

A content strategist has to wear many hats and assume many roles. What follows are 12 roles that the savvy strategist owns. Although you may not have the skills and experience to fulfill all of these roles today, use this list as a benchmark to work toward and to perfect over time. As you grow as a content strategist, you'll offer your clients greater insight, better skills and a bigger toolbox of resources and ideas.

1. Socially Connected

Your degree of popularity and influence in the social sphere greatly impacts your ability to drive content strategy. If your social voice and communication are not engaging to your friends, family and fans, then it's unlikely that you'll be able to create a voice for the business that will connect and convert. The best content strategists know how to engage readers and then re-engage them time and time again. Your ability to do this in the social sphere will spur shares and retweets of your posts that are like live reviews of your work and communication skills.

2. Story Finder and Teller

It's no secret: The best marketing tells a story. But consistently generating fresh, human-interest ideas for your content can be a struggle. The best content strategists, like the best journalists, have an instinct for finding and telling stories that both enlighten and entertain readers.

3. A/B and Multivariate Tester

Testing takes the guesswork out of website optimization and enables data-informed decisions that shift business conversations from "we think" to "we know." Content strategists know that by measuring the impact that changes have on your metrics, they can ensure that every change to content produces positive results.

4. Customer Journey Crafter

No one on the marketing team understands the customer more than a content strategist does. After all, it is strategists who develop the customer journey and who labor over the touch points defined by marketing, sales and customer service team members. It is strategists who have their fingers on the pulse of all content assets in the workflow that support those touch points. And it is strategists who take note of any gaps in the flow of content assets and who resolve to fill them with new content that will motivate customers at those stages of their journey.

5. Freelancer Orchestrator

Content strategists are only as good as the content assets they create and the results those content assets deliver. The demand for a wide variety of content assets makes it impossible for most companies to field a full-time team capable of delivering the goods. To plug the holes, an estimated 62 percent of companies outsource their content to freelance writers, designers, illustrators and photographers.

6. Detail Driver

For content strategists, it's all about the details — everything from content quality adherence to data harvesting to performance reporting. Even minor oversights in consideration of content strategy, your target audience and/or your management team could adversely affect reader retention, budgeting and ability to deliver on performance goals.

7. Ideation Guru

The ability to generate ideas — for content topics, marketing assets and even business betterment — is a key skill in a content strategist's bag of tricks. In the end, businesses with the best ideas, innovation and execution pathway win the content marketing war on the web. You'll need to keep the ideas coming and the creative juices flowing if you're going to take your content strategy career to the next level, and beyond.

8. Image Maker

You'll need not only to design the customer experience ecosystem but also to document it, telling stories with words, photographs and illustrations. Stories are the currency of marketing these days, for customers, stakeholders and all your readers and fans. It's up to you to describe your community in which they all live, to visualize what life is like at the company, or the conference, or just any random day that sheds light on the experience one would expect from joining the community or signing up with the service.

9. Socratic Learner

This could be my favorite paragraph in the workbook. Here's why: I learned early on in my business startup life that the question was the answer to just about any challenge I faced. The art of inquisitiveness is a must for anyone in business, but especially for those in sales and marketing. The more questions we ask, particularly the right questions, the more we learn about our customers, employees, thought leaders and friends. The more interested you are in them, the more interested they will be in you. Many selling techniques center on learning customer needs, and the only way to achieve that goal is by asking questions. The more knowledge we have about those needs, the more we can advise on the best solution, rather than preaching about our own products or services. So get Socratic: Stop selling. And start asking questions.

10. Sound Listener

Content marketing is defined as the art of listening to customers' wants and needs, and the science of creating and delivering informational content in response to those needs. The key to this definition lies in listening and learning about customers' wants and needs. Who better to turn to than those who hear from customers all day long — customer service representatives? These reps are an often overlooked resource for the marketing team. Don't make that same mistake. Learn firsthand from your customer service team what a customer is thinking, feeling and stating at every touch point in the customer journey.

11. Budget Wrangler

Take a closer look at the "performance" section of this workbook for more details about the many ways you can track the performance from your content marketing investment. The future of your company could rest with your ability to secure budgets from executives, board members and CFOs. Success in doing so starts with data that helps predict the future and with solid proposals crafted from experience.

12. Puzzle Maker

When it comes to puzzling out content strategy, there are many moving parts that need to come together. As content strategist, it is your job to prioritize the tasks and determine what actions can have the biggest impact on the business. It's easy to misplace one of the puzzle pieces: Content creation without research and planning will likely fail to deliver on performance goals. Likewise, failure to publish content consistently will diminish opportunities to connect with readers and the search engines. It's up to you, the content strategist, to put all the pieces of the puzzle together and deliver on the demands from the content marketing investment.

In a Nutshell

It's time to put it all together at WriterAccess, selecting the talent you need to achieve your goals from a small army of Writers, Editors, Content Strategists and Translators.

Exercise

Start cranking out great content with clear instructions that define what you need and what your audience demands to advance through their journey with you and your brand.

Certification Test

Then take the online Content Management Test.

CONTENT STRATEGY MASTERCLASS RESOURCE APPENDIX:

Welcome to your online GPS for content strategy -- WriterAccess. com/GamePlan. Open up a free account to access all the certification tests and resources to advance your content marketing career and grow your business organically — the content marketing way.

Content Marketing Tools

You'll download a copy of my "Top 139 Content Marketing Tools" book to get content strategy superpowers.

Content Planning Tools

BuzzSumo	Hootsuite	Quora
Answer the Public	GatherContent	Ripenn
Amazon Questions &	Hubspot	ScribbleLive
Answers	Blog Topic Generator	Social Animal
Basecamp	Jumpchart	Sprout Social
Co Schedule	Kapost	SurveyGizmo
DivvyHQ	Opal	Trello
Epictions	Ops Calendar	TweetDeck
		UXpin

Content Creation Tools

99 Designs	ClearVoice	Scripted
Adobe Creative Cloud	Contently	Textbroker
Audacity	GoAnimate	Visual.ly
Audience Ops	Piktochart	WriterAccess
Boost media	Prezi	Zerys
Canva	Qzzr	

Content Optimization Tools

Ahrefs
Brightinfo
Convert
Grammarbase
Grammarly
Hubspot
Influitive
Keyword Tool

Klout
Kred
Leadpages
Majestic
Moz
Optimizely
SEMrush
SiteTuners

Smartling
Sniply
SpyFu
SumoMe with Sumo
Unbounce
Visual Website Optimizer
WordStream
Wordtracker
Wordy

Content Distribution Tools

Act-On
BounceX
BrightCove
Constant Contact
ContentMX
Curata
Eventbrite
Facebook
Google+
GoToWebinar
Infusionsoft

Instagram
LinkedIn
MailChimp
Marketo
MyEmma
Oracle Eloqua
Ontraport
Outbrain
Pardot
Periscope
Pinterest

PR Newswire
PRWeb
ReadyTalk
Shareaholic
Silverpop
SnapApp
Snapchat
Taboola
Tumblr
Twitter
Uberflip
Youtube

Content Performance Tools

Adobe Analytics
Atomic Reach
Blitzmetrics
Crazy Egg
Google Analytics
Google Webmaster Tools

Hubspot Sales
KISSmetrics
mixpanel
Qualaroo
Raven Tools
SimpleReach

TrackMaven
Webtrends
Wistia
Woopra

Content Management Tools

Adobe Business Catalyst

Adobe Experience Manager

Blogger

Buffer

Canto

Content Launch

Contentful

Cvent

Double Dutch

Drupal

Joomla

LiveJournal

Newscred

Percussion

Rainmaker

Salesforce

Squarespace

Widen

WIX

WordPress

Content Marketing Blogs

Content Planning

- HubSpot (marketing blog) http://blog.hubspot.com/
- Moz https://moz.com/blog/the-ultimate-guide-to-content-planning
- CMI http://contentmarketinginstitute.com/developing-a-strategy/
- Uncommon.ly http://uncommonlysocial.com/one-page-content-marketing-plan/
- Find and Convert (FNC) http://www.findandconvert.com/blog
- Pam Didner Blog (influencer) http://pamdidner.com/blog/

Content Creation

- Vertical Measures http://www.verticalmeasures.com/content/how-to-create-awesome-content-people-actually-want-071916/
- QuickSprout https://www.quicksprout.com/2015/08/21/18-tools-for-better-content-creation-improve-your-writing-with-less-effort/
- Buzzsumo http://buzzsumo.com/blog/
- Intentional Design http://intentionaldesign.ca/
- Jeff Bullas Blog (influencer) http://www.jeffbullas.com/
- Ann Handley http://www.annhandley.com/blog/

Content Optimization
- Vertical Measures http://www.verticalmeasures.com/content-marketing-2/12-content-optimization-tips-to-avoid-common-seo-issues-071216/
- Inbound Marketing Agents http://www.inboundmarketingagents.com/inbound-marketing-agents-blog
- Buzzsumo http://buzzsumo.com/blog/
- Cynthia Johnson (Influencer) http://www.cynthialive.com/blog
- Maximize Your Social (Neal Schaffer) http://maximizeyoursocial.com/blog/
- InFlow http://www.goinflow.com/blog/
- HubSpot http://blog.hubspot.com/

Content Distribution
- Buffer Blog https://blog.bufferapp.com/content-distribution-tools
- HubSpot http://blog.hubspot.com/
- Social Media Examiner http://www.socialmediaexaminer.com/
- Marketo (E-mail Marketing Blog) http://blog.marketo.com/category/email-marketing
- RightHello http://righthello.com/blog/
- Campaign Monitor https://www.campaignmonitor.com/blog/
- Marketing Profs http://www.marketingprofs.com/marketing/library/articles/

Content Performance
- Kissmetrics https://blog.kissmetrics.com/ "A blog about analytics, marketing and testing"
- Moz https://moz.com/Blog
- Convice & Convert - Social Media Measurement Blog http://www.convinceandconvert.com/category/social-media-measurement/
- TopRank Blog http://www.toprankblog.com/category/seo/

- Social Media Examiner http://www.socialmediaexaminer.com/
- Brian Honigman Blog (Influencer) http://www.brianhonigman.com/blog/
- InFlow http://www.goinflow.com/blog/
- HubSpot http://blog.hubspot.com/

Content Management
- HubSpot http://blog.hubspot.com/
- Intentional Design http://intentionaldesign.ca/
- Gadgetopia http://gadgetopia.com/
- CMS Myth http://www.cmsmyth.com/

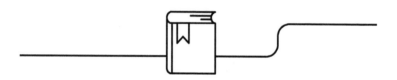

Content Marketing Books and e-Books

Content Planning
- "The Content Marketing Book of Answers: Strategy & Planning" by Jodi Harris
- "Buyer Personas: How to Gain Insight into Your Customer's Expectations, Align Your Marketing Strategies, and Win More Business" by Adele Revella
- "Content Inc.: How Entrepreneurs Use Content to Build Massive Audiences and Create Radically Successful Businesses" by Joe Pulizzi
- Hubspot e-book : "A Practical Guide to Building a Killer Content Strategy" http://offers.hubspot.com/a-practical-guide-to-building-a-killer-content-strategy
- CMI e-book: "Launch Your Own Content Marketing Program: Why, Who, & How" http://contentmarketinginstitute.com/launch-content-marketing-program/

- "The 2015 Chief Marketing Officer Handbook: Marketing Strategies That Work" by Invert
- "The CMO's Periodic Table: A Renegade's Guide to Marketing (Voices That Matter)" by Drew Neisser
- "The Cmo's Social Media Handbook: A Step-By-Step Guide for Leading Marketing Teams in the Social Media World" by Peter Friedman

Content Creation
- "The Content Strategy Toolkit: Methods, Guidelines, and Templates for Getting Content Right" by Meghan Casey
- "Meaningful: The Story of Ideas That Fly" by Bernadette Jiwa
- "Epic Content Marketing: How to Tell a Different Story, Break through the Clutter, and Win More Customers by Marketing Less" by Joe Pulizzi
- "Content Rules: How to Create Killer Blogs, Podcasts, Videos, e-books, Webinars (and More) That Engage Customers and Ignite Your Business" by Ann Handley and C.C. Chapman
- Hubspot e-book: "How to Build a Content Creation Process for Your Marketing Agency" http://offers.hubspot.com/build-content-creation-process
- HubSpot Content Creation Kit (4 e-books, 1 webinar, 1 template) http://offers.hubspot.com/content-creation-kit
- Copyblogger e-book: "Copywriting 101: How to craft compelling copy" http://www.copyblogger.com/copywriting-101/
- "Sisomo: The Future on Screen" by Kevin Roberts, https://www.amazon.com/Sisomo-Future-Screen-Kevin-Roberts/dp/1576872688
- "Unconscious Branding: How Neuroscience Can Empower (and Inspire) Marketing" by Douglas Van Praet, https://www.amazon.com/Unconscious-Branding-Neuroscience-Empower-Marketing/dp/1137278927/
- "The Storyteller's Secret" by Carmine Gallo, https://www.amazon.com/Storytellers-Secret-Speakers-Business-Legends/dp/1250071550/

- "The Paradox of Choice: Why More Is Less" by Barry Schwartz, https://smile.amazon.com/Paradox-Choice-Why-More-Less/dp/0060005696/
- "Story: Substance, Structure, Style and the Principles of Screenwriting" by Robert McKee, https://smile.amazon.com/Story-Substance-Structure-Principles-Screenwriting/dp/0060391685/
- "The Write-Brain Workbook" by Bonnie Neubauer, https://smile.amazon.com/Write-Brain-Workbook-Revised-Expanded-Exercises/dp/159963838

Content Optimization

- Yoast e-book — "Content SEO" by Marieke van de Rakt and Joost de Valk https://yoast.com/ebooks/content-seo-2/
- "The Art of SEO: Mastering Search Engine Optimization," 3rd Edition by Eric Enge, Stephan Spencer and Jessie Stricchiola
- "SEO Fitness Workbook, 2016 Edition: The Seven Steps to Search Engine Optimization Success on Google" by Jason McDonald, Ph.D.
- "Optimize: How to Attract and Engage More Customers by Integrating SEO, Social Media, and Content Marketing" by Lee Odden
- Tone e-book: "Understanding SEO techniques" https://www.tone.co.uk/ebook/understanding-seo-techniques/
- Optimizely e-book: "Optimization Survival Guide" http://pages.optimizely.com/optimization-survival-guide.html
- Optimizely e-book: "Optimization Benchmark" http://pages.optimizely.com/wp-benchmark-survey.html
- "Earn It, Don't Buy It: The CMO's Guide to Social Media Marketing in a Post Facebook World" by Jim Tobin

Content Distribution

- "Non Obvious: How to Think Different, Curate Ideas & Predict the Future" by Rohit Bhargava
- "The Art of Impact: How to Use Content Marketing the Right Way to Build Your Brand, Grow Your Business and Make a

Difference" by Pam Hendrickson
- Coschedule e-book: "How to Distribute Your Content to Reach More People" by Nathan Ellering http://coschedule.com/blog/content-distribution/
- Curata e-book: "Content Marketing Done Right" http://www.curata.com/resources/ebooks/content-marketing-done-right
- Relevance e-book: "Quick guide for content promotion" https://www.publi.sh/content-details/quick-guide-for-content-promotion
- Curata e-book: "Content Curation Lookbook" http://www.curata.com/resources/ebooks/content-curation-look-book
- "Curate This: The Hands-on, How-to Guide to Content Curation" by Steven Rosenbaum
- "Email Marketing Rules: A Step-by-Step Guide to the Best Practices That Power Email Marketing Success" by Chad White and Jay Baer
- "Email Persuasion: Captivate and Engage Your Audience, Build Authority and Generate More Sales With Email Marketing" by Ian Brodie

Content Performance
- "Web Analytics: An Hour a Day" by Avinash Kaushik
- "Data-Driven Marketing: The 15 Metrics Everyone in Marketing Should Know" by Mark Jeffery
- "Digital Marketing Analytics: Making Sense of Consumer Data in a Digital World" by Chuck Hemann and Ken Burbary
- Uberflip e-book: "Data-Driven Content Marketing" by Hana Abaza http://hub.uberflip.com/h/i/44513860-data-driven-content-marketing-ebook
- CMI e-book: "A Field Guide to the 4 Types of Content Marketing Metrics" http://contentmarketinginstitute.com/2012/11/a-field-guide-to-the-4-types-of-content-marketing-metrics-ebook/
- "The CRM Handbook: A Business Guide to Customer Relationship Management" by Jill Dyché

Content Management

- "Managing Enterprise Content: A Unified Content Strategy" (2nd Edition) (Voices That Matter) by Ann Rockley and Charles Cooper
- Marketo e-book: "How to Build and Operate a Content Marketing Machine" https://www.marketo.com/ebooks/build-and-operate-content-marketing-machine/
- QuickSprout e-book: "The Advanced Guide to Content Marketing" by Neil Patel and Kathryn Aragon https://www.quicksprout.com/the-advanced-guide-to-content-marketing/
- Bridgeline Digital e-book: "Give Your CMS an SEO Jolt" http://www.bridgelinedigital.com/resource-center/ebooks/give-your-cms-an-seo-jolt
- "Web Content Management: Systems, Features, and Best Practices" by Deane Barker
- "Content Strategy for the Web," 2nd edition by Kristina Halvorson and Melissa Rach

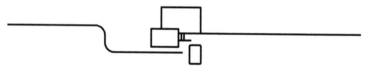

Content Marketing Web Articles

Content Strategy

- "The History of Content Marketing," infographic, Content Marketing Institute, http://contentmarketinginstitute.com/2016/07/history-content-marketing/
- "B2B Content Marketing: 2016 Benchmarks, Budgets and Trends—North America," Content Marketing Institute, http://contentmarketinginstitute.com/wp-content/uploads/2015/09/2016_B2B_Report_Final.pdf
- "Content Marketing History," infographic, Curata, http://www.curata.com/blog/content-marketing-history-infographic/
- "World Wide Web Timeline," Pew Research Center, http://www.pewinternet.org/2014/03/11/world-wide-web-timeline/

- "Customer Acquisition vs. Retention Costs—Statistics And Trends," infographic, invesp, http://www.invespcro.com/blog/customer-acquisition-retention/

Content Planning
- "20 Questions to Ask When Creating Buyer Personas," free template, HubSpot, http://blog.hubspot.com/blog/tabid/6307/bid/30907/9-Questions-You-Need-to-Ask-When-Developing-Buyer-Personas.aspx#sm.00001bjbuiypada6s3f2kmf895pse
- "Marketing Multipliers: 7 Remarkable Ways to Sell Without Selling," WriterAccess, http://www.writeraccess.com/webinar-archive/marketing-multipliers-7-ways-sell-without-selling/

Content Creation
- "Make Your Content Snap, Crackle, Pop," video, WriterAccess, https://www.youtube.com/watch?v=fm1fLWmL_0U
- "6 Ways To Increase User Engagement On Your Content," Jayson DeMers, Forbes.com, http://www.forbes.com/sites/jaysondemers/2016/05/07/6-ways-to-increase-user-engagement-on-your-content/#75706377907f
- "Why Creativity and Emotion Matter Most," webinar, Douglas Van Praet, WriterAccess, http://www.writeraccess.com/webinar-archive/why-creativity-emotion-matter-most/
- "Neuromarketing: The Brainy Path to Persuasive Content," webinar, Roger Dooley, WriterAccess, http://www.writeraccess.com/webinar-archive/neuromarketing-brainy-path-persuasive-content/
- How B2B Content Impacts Buying Decisions," infographic, MarketingProfs, http://www.marketingprofs.com/charts/2013/10888/how-b2b-content-impacts-buying-decisions-infographic
- "Storytelling 101: How to Seize the Attention of a Distracted Audience," Barry Feldman, HubSpot, http://blog.hubspot.com/marketing/how-to-seize-attention-of-distracted-audience-ht#sm.00001bjbuiypada6s3f2kmf895pse
- CMO Council Study https://www.cmocouncil.org/press-detail.php?id=4481

Content Optimization

- "SEO Simplified for Short Attention Spans: Learn the Essentials of Search Engine Optimization in Under an Hour" by Barry Feldman, https://www.amazon.com/SEO-Simplified-Short-Attention-Spans/dp/1518822207
- "The Periodic Table Of SEO Success Factors," infographic, http://searchengineland.com/seotable
- "9 Actionable Tips to Build An Effective Lead Magnet," VWO blog, https://vwo.com/blog/9-tips-effective-lead-magnet/

Content Distribution

- "50+ Places to Repurpose Your Content: The Ultimate Guide," CoSchedule, http://coschedule.com/blog/repurpose-your-content/
- Facebook Advertiser Help Center, https://www.facebook.com/business/help/547448218658012
- LinkedIn Marketing Solutions, https://business.linkedin.com/marketing-solutions
- "Start Advertising on YouTube," https://www.youtube.com/yt/advertise/
- "Google Display Specifications," https://support.google.com/displayspecs#topic=4588474
- "12 Examples of Native Ads (And Why They Work)," Copyblogger, http://www.copyblogger.com/examples-of-native-ads/
- Taboola home page, http://www.taboola.com/
- Adblade home page, https://adblade.com/
- Outbrain home page, http://www.outbrain.com/
- StumbleUpon home page, http://ads.stumbleupon.com/
- Reddit home page, https://www.reddit.com/advertising/
- "Survey: 90% Of Customers Say Buying Decisions Are Influenced By Online Reviews," Marketing Land, http://marketingland.com/survey-customers-more-frustrated-by-how-long-it-takes-to-resolve-a-customer-service-issue-than-

the-resolution-38756
- "30 Action Items to Get Serious About Influencer Marketing," Feldman Creative, http://feldmancreative.com/2014/08/influencer-marketing-action-items/
- "22 Influencer Marketing Ideas From Influential Marketers," infographic, http://blog.hubspot.com/marketing/influencer-marketing-ideas-infographic#sm.00001bjbuiypada6s3f2kmf895pse

Content Performance
- "Content, Shares, and Links: Insights from Analyzing 1 Million Articles," Moz, https://moz.com/blog/content-shares-and-links-insights-from-analyzing-1-million-articles
- "The Magical Content that Gets Links and Shares – New Research," BuzzSumo, http://buzzsumo.com/blog/magical-content-gets-links-shares-new-research-buzzsumo-majestic/
- "Customer Acquisition Cost: The One Metric That Can Determine Your Company's Fate," KissMetrics blog, https://blog.kissmetrics.com/customer-acquisition-cost/

Past Content Marketing Conference Speakers

Name	Blog
AJ Wilcox	**b2linked.com**
Amisha Gandhi	linkedin.com/in/amisha-gandhi-a6534b1
Andrew Davis	**akadrewdavis.com**
Andy Crestodina	orbitmedia.com
Ann Handley	**annhandley.com**
Anum Hussain	anumhussain.com
Aparna Nancherla	**aparnacomedy.com**
Arnie Kuenn	verticalmeasures.com
Ayat Shukairy	**invespcro.com/blog/ayat-shukairy**
Bill Carmody	billcarmody.com
Brandy Lawson	**fieryfx.com**
Brian Halligan	blog.hubspot.com
Bryan Kramer	**bryankramer.com**
Byron White	writeraccess.com
Chad Pollitt	**chadpollitt.com**
Chelsey Delaney	catalystnyc.com
Chris Dayley	**disruptiveadvertising.com**
Christina Inge	christinainge.com
Colin Eagan	**colineagan.com**
David Nihill	7comedyhabits.com
Doug Kessler	**velocitypartners.com**
Erica McGillivray	sliverofice.com
Francesca Fiorentini	**francescafiorentini.com**
Greg Roth	theideaenthusiast.com
Greg Stuart	**vdestination.com**
Hana Abaza	hanaabaza.comv
Heather Dopson	**heatherdopson.com**

Name	Blog
Heidi Cohen	actionablemarketingguide.com
Inbar Yagur	**taboola.com**
Jason Falls	jasonfalls.com/blog
Jenn LeBlanc	**linkedin.com/in/jenniferleblanc**
Jessica Best	emarketingplatform.com
Jill Grozalsky	**cmswire.com**
Joe Lazauskas	linkedin.com/in/joe-lazauskas-8b442026
Joe Pulizzi	**contentmarketinginstitute.com**
John Hall	johnhallspeaker.com
Jon Burkhart	**jon-burkhart.squarespace.com**
Jonathan Kranz	kranzcom.com
Josh Bernoff	**withoutbullshit.com**
Josh Steimle	joshsteimle.com
Justin Rondeau	**digitalmarketer.com**
Katie Farrer	ibm.com
Katie Martell	**katie-martell.com**
Larry Kim	blog.hubspot.com
Lee Odden	**toprankblog.com**
Lindsay Marder	digitalmarketer.com
Luna Malbroux	**lunaisamerica.com**
Margaret Magnarelli	linkedin.com/in/margaretmagnarelli
Margot Bloomstein	**fullscreendirect.com**
Marilyn Cox	mmmatters.com
Matthew Barby	**matthewbarby.com**
Melanie Deziel	mdeziel.com
Michael Brenner	**marketinginsidergroup.com**
Mike Roberts	linkedin.com/in/mrspy
Nadya Khoja	**thisisnadya.com**
Nancy Harhut	wildeagency.com
Neal Schaffer	**nealschaffer.com**
Nikoletta Vecsei Harrold	thecontentwrangler.com
Norm Laviolette	**normlaviolette.com**

Name	Blog
Pam Didner	pamdidner.com
Paul Roetzer	**performance.pr2020.com**
Pawan Deshpande	curata.com
Peter McGraw	**petermcgraw.org**
Rachel Meyer	supershuttle.com
Rebecca Lieb	**rebeccalieb.com**
Robert Rose	robertrose.net
Ron Tite	**rontite.com**
Sam Martin	leafly.com
Samantha Stone	**marketingadvisorynetwork.com**
Sandra Matz	sandramatz.com
Sarah Cooper	**thecooperreview.com**
Sarah Hill	storyup.com
Sarah Wiese	**sarahweise.com**
Scott Abel	thecontentwrangler.com
Spencer Smith	**spencerxsmith.com**
Steve Rayson	buzzsumo.com
Sweta Patel	**swetaspeaks.com**
Taylor Rose	linkedin.com/in/taylorrose
Tim Ash	**sitetuners.com**
Tim Washer	timwasher.com
Travis Wright	**traviswright.com**
Tyler Lessard	salesforce.com
Veronica Romney	**losomoinc.com**
Vesselin Popov	rgnn.org/author/vesselin-popov

CPSIA information can be obtained
at www.ICGtesting.com
Printed in the USA
FFHW01n1843280918
48591676-52514FF